SOULmate PROPRIETORS

How To Run A Business with Your Spouse and STAY Married!

DANELLE BROWN

SOULmate Proprietors
How to Run a Business with Your Spouse and Stay Married

By Danelle Brown

Queen Bee Consulting

Published by Queen Bee Consulting, Glen Carbon, Illinois, USA

Copyeditor: Lori Zue Stevens, www.lorizueedits.com; Cover and interior design: Jack & Cathy Davis, Davis Creative, www.DavisCreative.com; Cover copy: Cathy Davis, Davis Creative, www.DavisCreative.com

Library of Congress Cataloging-in-Publication Data
Library of Congress Control Number: 2010911717

Danelle Brown
SOULmate Proprietors: How to Run a Business with Your Spouse and Stay Married

ISBN: 978098292570-6

Library of Congress subject headings:
1. Business 2. Heading Listing 3. Heading Listing
CIP Number 2011

To my wonderful daughters, Isabella and Elena,
who make me want to be a better person every day.

To my husband, Marcel, this book would not exist without your
love, friendship, and support.

And to husbands and wives that work together — I truly hope
this book helps you keep your dream alive.

I dedicate this book to all of you.

SOULmate Proprietors

Acknowledgments

Thank you is not a strong enough statement to express my appreciation. I never would have accomplished this if it were not for so many people encouraging me and supporting me through the entire process.

The first step, however, is to thank the wonderful woman who approached me about writing this book in the first place: Karen Hoffman. You are an inspiration and a role model, demonstrating every day what every business owner should be. You never stopped believing in me and being a cheerleader to share my talents with the world. Thank you so much, Karen.

Thanks, also, to my eWomen Network friends; Donna Gamache, for running such a fabulous group of networking ladies and for promoting me every chance she gets; Linda Kluge, for giving me a swift kick in the butt to get this project done; and to Carrie Silver-Stock, who gave me countless hours of advice and answers on how to be a coach and an author. Don't know where I would be without your support, ladies!

Thank you to Jan King, who continues to stand by me as I progress as an author. She has always given me great advice and cheered me on from the moment we first met and she heard my book idea. To Cathy Davis, for always giving me great advice on being an author and about the world of publishing, and, basically, for holding my hand all the time, and to Lori Zue, the world's best editor. I can't believe we managed to tame my thoughts into a wonderful work of art other people can understand.

To the stars of my book, Mark and Pat Slaughter, Andy and Kathy Bridgeman, Barry and Melissa DeLassus, Lee Horvath and Christy Gan, Dino and Jules Karagiannis, Dan and Julie Lohmann—I salute you. Thank you for being brave and honest and for sharing such an important part of yourselves and your family to educate the world. Thank you, as well, to every couple I questioned, interviewed or got nosey with. Your answers shaped many details of this book, and I wish I could have included every one of you.

To the members of my very first Mastermind Group—Dana Klassen, Ed Faller, Ryan High, Ryan Matthews and Christy Gan—who have stuck with me for the past three years. Thanks to you, I feel lucky every day to have my job. I am pleased to not only have you as clients but as friends.

To Michael Port, Elizabeth Marshall, Rob Thomas, Lou Bortone, Brent Burns, Thomas Mangum, Cindy Earl and Megan McKenzie: the Book Yourself Solid team that helped make me the coach I am today. I am forever grateful for your advice and knowledge.

To the members of the Edwardsville/Glen Carbon Chamber of Commerce—you took Marcel and me into your fold and guided us through our early years, helping us become respected business owners. A special thanks to the staff: Carol Foreman, Linda Daniels, Bonnie Kotsybar, Desiree Bennyhoff—thank you for your help and friendship.

A huge thank you to my loving family. My mom, who gave me endless encouragement and praise; my sister Paula, who always helped with my girls when I needed to work or write; and my two adorable daughters, Isabella and Elena, who, even at their young age, inspire me daily and did their best to be good while I was writing. I love you both so very much. I never would have finished this project without seeing your smiles every day.

And most of all, to my wonderful husband, Marcel. Without you, none of this would have been imaginable, feasible or possible. You bring out the best in me and I am proud of what we have accomplished together. Thank you for always being there, putting up with me from start to finish and being my biggest cheerleader. I am everything I am because of your faith and love. I love you more than words can say.

SOULmate Proprietors

Testimonials

"Soulmate Proprietors is a must read for every couple currently working together and those who are considering it. I have coached many business owners, many of whom are husband and wife teams. I can honestly say that any couple applying the principles in this book will strengthen their personal and business relationships, which will make their business more successful. Danelle does an excellent job of getting to the core of this unique business arrangement and using real world examples focused on making couple-run businesses thrive. She thinks big and gives couples the ability to take her advice and run with it. If you are serious about running a successful business with your spouse, this is the book for you."

Michael Port
New York Times Bestselling Author of 4 Books including "Book Yourself Solid" and "Think Big Manifesto"

"Danelle Brown is an amazing woman! This book is timely in that my husband and I are working together to help individuals create a Powerful Business Presence through visual image, photography and video. We look forward to learning how to succeed in this joint venture and still keep our marriage alive and well. Thank you Danelle for giving this book to the world!"

Donna Gamache
www.DonnaGamache.com
Business Presence Expert

Compatible in the bedroom and curious if you are compatible in the boardroom? Danelle Brown's new book Soulmate Proprietors: How To Run A Business With Your Spouse and STAY Married gives you long-lasting tools for partners at work and home. Her book goes beyond exploring the obvious ramifications—it's a valuable and practical guide for anyone that is thinking about or currently working with their spouse.

—Sharon Sayler author of *What Your Body Says (And How to Master the Message): Inspire, Influence, Build Trust, and Create Lasting Business Relationships*

Danelle Brown has the gift of being smart, business savvy and fun. Couples building a business together can be challenged, and Danelle helps couples figure out how to be happy and profitable business partners while keeping their marriage a priority. As someone who is in business with her spouse, Marcel, she knows her subject matter well! I always, always enjoy bouncing ideas off this incredibly connected lady.

Karen Hoffman-Your Dream Champion
Co-founder of "City of Experts" and author of *The Art of Barter-How to Trade for Almost Anything*

"I have been in business with my spouse for 10 years and counting, and I can tell you there are not enough books about this complicated topic. I wish I had the knowledge and tips from this book years ago. SoulMate Proprietors really tackles the issues that married couples will face when working together! I highly recommend this book to any couple who is just starting a business together or are already working together. It is full of helpful ideas and strategies for making this unique working relationship both productive and rewarding."

Sandra Yancey, Founder and CEO, eWomenNetwork, Inc.

Contents

SOULmate Proprietors

Introduction

You've decided to open your own business. Awesome! Best of all, you've decided to do this with your spouse. Congratulations on your decision, because I doubt it was an easy feat. Whatever happened in your life to get you to this decision, I applaud you.

A husband-and-wife team is an increasingly common business dynamic. My husband and I have thrived in our business partnership for more than thirteen years, yet most people view us with part awe, part skepticism and part shock, as if there were a magical formula that renders possible the tantalizing idea of working with a spouse.

With humor and common sense and the advice of many couples I have interviewed, I will show you how to accomplish this while still enjoying the respect, love and admiration that brought you together in the first place. I include fun, light-hearted, useful, real-world advice and tips for success. Six couples share their misadventures and triumphs, and I believe you'll relate to their stories and love them for their generosity.

The number of couple-owned businesses in the country is rising as people choose to make changes about their careers, due to the economy or to work/life balance issues. Both men and women are increasingly curious about the dynamics of working with a spouse. Yet no one teaches this subject in school, and our ancestors' knowledge—be they mercantile owners or farmers—was not passed on. Without fail, when people find out my husband and I run a successful business, they comment, "How do you work with your spouse? I would have killed mine by now!"

But who says I haven't?! No, of course I haven't, although there were certainly times in the early days when we could have walked away from the business, or our marriage, or both, and this is what people fear the most. Soulmate Proprietors provides the keys to successfully managing both a business and a marriage. Through experience and research—often trial and error—from my husband and I, plus that from other husband-and-wife teams, I've gathered relatable anecdotes and practical advice that readers can implement immediately.

"I can't imagine working any other way. I love my husband and feel lucky we work together every day to achieve a common goal." This sentiment was shared by many of the couples I interviewed. I firmly believe this, and most other husband-and-wife teams do too. I interviewed dozens of couples, and I'm excited to share their amazing insights and hard-earned knowledge with you. My only lament is that I could not feature every one of them. The couples spotlighted in this book each had several points that resonated with me or perfectly helped me make a particular point. But all the couples I interviewed contributed greatly to this book.

I am on a mission to debunk a common misconception: Your spouse would make a poor business partner. The reality is spouses are probably one of the best options. With hundreds of people laid off each day, this may be the best time to develop that partnership. If you start a business, it's likely your spouse will be involved anyway, either financially or as an extra set of hands. Who better than someone who has your best interests at heart to be a business partner? Many successful companies that positively impact our economy were founded in a spare bedroom, home office or garage—and were lucky enough to be run by spouses who supported, encouraged and participated in each other's dreams.

Now it is your turn. So, let's get started on your dream!

Chapter
One

*Build your business around your passion,
not the other way around.*

David Siteman Garland, author of
*Smarter, Faster, Cheaper, Non-Boring,
Fluff-free Strategies for Marketing and
Promoting Your Business*

In It to Win It

How Much Do You Love Me?

There are a few things that can really test a marriage. Running a business together is certainly one of them, like almost no other endeavor.

If you want to run a business with your spouse, you must realize that you are building the business on a foundation that is your marriage. Like any structure, your business will only be as strong as its foundation. Is your relationship strong enough to handle spending a lot of time together? Is your marriage strong enough to be the foundation of a business? Can you compromise with your spouse? Do you both have the right mindset to handle the stress and pressure that come with business ownership? Can you both respect each other's strengths and weaknesses and work together to maximize each other's potential?

Ideally, these questions and more should be carefully evaluated and answered before entering into a business together. If you are already in a business together, there is no time like the present to review these concepts and see if there is room for improvement.

Let's start with simple questions that revolve around your personalities. Do you get along when you are together a lot? Some of you may laugh at this, but it is a legitimate question. If you don't get along when you spend time together and you don't really have a strong marriage to begin with, don't even think about running a business together. Don't overlook this point—it's fundamental and a key to making both your marriage and your business succeed.

Most people assume that married couples naturally get along—of course they do, right? But do they get along 95 percent of the time? I know a lot of couples who constantly bicker. Can you imagine implementing a business in the middle of that kind of behavior? I would probably kill them if I worked there!

It's also important to know that certain dynamics in your relationship will change as the business evolves. Even though this is not necessarily a bad thing, change can frighten some people. Regardless of your firm belief that the two of you would never let anything come between you, you must consider if you have a strong enough foundation to deal with the changing dynamics, for starters.

Ask yourselves these questions about the type and strength of your relationship:

> How well do you *really* get along?
>
> Do you like each other all that much?
>
> Do you have a solid relationship now?
>
> As you think about the person you will be working with every day, and then see at home every night, do you feel excited or scared?

Most people, when they heard I was going to write this book, starting laughing. Not at me, but at the thought of working with their spouse. Most of them say, "You must have the patience of a saint to pull that off every day," when they find out how long my husband and I have been running a business together. This attitude is exactly what I am talking about: If you cannot hang out in the same room with one another for eight-plus hours a day, often in the midst of stressful times, then don't go down the business road until you have had the time and experience together as a couple to get a handle on that.

This was not an issue for my husband and me. We were friends first, before we ever dated or got married. We got along very well and enjoyed spending time with each other. That's not to say we didn't have our moments occasionally, and we still do, but we agreed early on about what we wanted from our marriage and from our business. In terms of our relationship as a couple, we were prepared—as well as anyone can be—to handle and deal with the daily challenges of running a business together.

Use Your Backbone to Bend

Can you compromise? This is another big question that gets skipped in the beginning. It's a tricky one.

I have to admit, both then and now, that I am the strong-willed one in our relationship. Like most people, I didn't really like it when I didn't get my way. In the beginning of our relationship, I was constantly battling for things to go according to *my* vision, and I brought this expectation and need into the business relationship too. It caused a lot of unnecessary grief. Compromise is definitely not a one-way street, I eventually learned.

The concept of compromise was an issue with a lot of the couples I interviewed. Power struggles, endless discussions, the fear of looking bad in front of someone—these all make it difficult to compromise. It's challenging to give up a little ground when you truly believe in your point of view. Usually only one decision can be made, however, so compromise is necessary.

5 Tips to Get from Stalemate to Compromise

- **Be honest about your own shortcomings**

- **Think about the bigger picture—what will you gain from pushing this issue?**

- **Have each person make a list of pros and cons pertinent to the situation that reflect his or her point of view**

- **Sleep on it**

- **If a fifty-fifty compromise is impossible, lean toward the person with more experience**

Compromise means listening to both sides and making a decision on which way to go. You have to trust your partner's abilities and be able to bend from time to time. Both of you will have to bend on issues sooner or later. Each one of you will have to give in at some point.

So drop the attitude of "my way or the highway" or feeling like you know what is best. Don't let fear, anger and frustration rule which way you will decide. Go with the person who has the most experience or ability to deal with that issue and trust his or her judgment. (We will talk more about division of roles in chapter two.)

I can guarantee there will be disagreements on money, marketing, timing, family commitments and many other things, too. My advice is to pick your battles and give in on others. The ability to compromise will get you through your struggles.

A Different Bundle of Joy

For you parents out there, do you remember what it was like to bring home a baby? By the time you actually do walk in the door with your newborn, you've had to make many decisions together. Where will the nursery be in the house? What color will we paint the room? When you registered at a store for all things baby, so your friends and family would know what to give you, how did you and your spouse select these items? And don't forget the constant pre-natal visits to the doctor to check on the health of the baby. Adoptive parents often have an even harder time as they wait and wonder and worry—which can lead to second-guessing their decisions and longer debates to eventually arrive at new ones.

At last, your bundle of joy is here. You bring him or her home and now there is still more to learn: feeding, changing, sleeping habits, new schedules and learning even more time-management skills to keep the household running. It continues as your bundle of joy grows, with decisions on such topics as selecting playmates, activities, schools, driving schedules, and who will help constantly nurture your little bundle as he or she grows.

Having a business with your spouse is like having your first baby. Typically, neither adult has done this before, so you are learning together how everything works. The baby and the business need constant attention, nurturing and guiding, and they cannot be left alone in the early years. Think about it. You are building your empire from scratch and most of the time you are the only one who knows what is going on or how to handle problems if they come up. My husband and I were constantly looking to each other for answers when it came to the baby or our business—hoping the other had the answer even though neither of us had never done this before!

The first years are always the hardest in a business: establishing roles, learning how to deal with rules and regulations, what to do when you face adversity, who is in charge when you can't be there. Just like a baby, you are dealing with your business 24/7. Just like taking turns to get up in the middle of the night to feed the baby, you will each bring the business home with you. It will take over dinner conversation, keep you awake at night, and all events previously thought of as "family outings" will now be centered around what is going on with the business.

How do you decide whose turn it is to get up in the middle of the night with the business?

Just like having a baby together, however, the rewards of owning a business together are great. The chance to have built and be in charge of something that is significant to you and other people outweighs the risk and work.

But let's back up and not gloss over this point: You will bring the business home with you. It does not matter where the business is located—if it's a home-based business you run out of your spare room or outbuildings, or you have office space or a storefront. You will eat, sleep and breathe the business. It is inevitable. So whatever your business is, you'd better be comfortable talking about it at home. A lot of people think that just because it is time to go home, all business dealings should stop. Not true in a spouse-run business. Oftentimes, dinner is your first opportunity to sit and think without interruption. If one of you is out of the office during the day, selling or performing work for the business, dinnertime or the evening is your only chance to discuss what went on during the day.

All of my couples said "you'd better be okay with talking business at home." I agree with them. My husband and I have had many quick discussions while brushing our teeth, or held a business meeting once we finally put the kids to bed, or woke up in the morning and quickly figured out our schedules for the day.

And it's not just the talking that gets done at home, but also the actual work you do—your duties within the business. Maybe you bring it home on your computer, or even stick it in the back drawer of your brain while you're with your family, but you still have to get it done—at home, because it didn't get done during the day—so the bills can get paid.

Know this going in: There is no on/off switch. The business follows you.

4 Rules for at Home—and Keeping Everyone Happy:

1. **Don't complain about the need to talk business at home, and do maintain a positive attitude.**

2. **Respect the other person's decision when he or she does not want to talk shop at home.**

3. **Be mindful of overdoing it, and don't let it rule your life.**

4. **Keep it constructive. Don't say "you should have" or point fingers.**

What Do You Want to Be When You Grow Up?

What is your business going to be about? I have often heard people get into a certain line of work because "they fell into it."

Or maybe they have a certain knack for doing something so they find a job because it was easy and obvious.

Let's use me as an example. In high school, I was good with numbers and being organized. I did very well in my business and accounting classes, so everyone said I should be an accountant. Not knowing any better, that is what I planned to do as I started college. I quickly learned, however, that this was not what I wanted my life to be. Don't get me wrong: Being good with numbers and being organized are great skills to have, but I was not passionate about being an accountant, specifically. I was not excited about getting up every day to worry about debits and credits. I have met people who are excited about numbers—more power to them. They are doing exactly what they should be doing: running successful accounting practices.

My husband once asked me if money were no object, what would I want to do with my life? He encouraged me to go out and learn how to do it for a living.

My answer was that I love talking to people. I love helping people. Marketing, promoting and coaching do not feel like work to me. I love it, so it was a natural move for me to take on that role in our business.

In my husband's case, he loves computers and technology. I mean loves. Did I say LOVES? I just want to make that very

clear. He loves it all. And as technology evolved, his love for it
has simply evolved and grown right along with it. He is as giddy
as a schoolboy when he learns about new technologies and ways
to use them to benefit people. He thrives on helping business
owners harness technology and use it to make their lives easier,
not harder. I remember the first time he got paid when he helped
someone fix a computer. He came home with $50 in his pocket
and we thought, "Whoa, we can get paid to do this?"

We have taken our skills and combined them to create a great
business that satisfies a specific need in the business world.

And so it can be with you. What are you passionate about? This
is not necessarily what you are good at, although they often go
hand in hand. Remember my accounting background: I certainly
use it today to be successful, but it is not where my passion lies.
What does not feel like work to you? What makes you so happy
that you can easily get out of bed every day and go do it? Is there
something you do that you love and just can't believe you are
getting paid to do it—or *could* get paid to do it?

Think about how you can combine your passion and talents with
those of your spouse so the two of you can take on the world and
bring us something no one else has. Capitalize on your strengths
and use them to build a business that makes you happy. If you
don't have passion for what you do, you will not be successful.

What Does "In It to Win It" Mean?

So what do I mean when I say "in it to win it"? I often use this phrase when I am referring to my clients who have extreme dedication, drive and vision. They want to be the best at what they do, to think outside of the box, and roll with and overcome adversity. They want to think bigger, reinvent the way things are done, give back to their communities, and take on larger competitors doing it bigger, better or more creatively. Being in it to win it is just that. Running a business, even on your own, takes a lot of work. Add in the dynamic of a spouse and it can get more complicated. Dedication to the business has to be there. When both of you are involved in the company and your family relies on the business's revenue, you have to be willing to work smarter, harder and faster, and be ready to embrace and run with the vision that got you here in the first place. One of my couples said, "Be prepared to work your ass off for it." That pretty much sums it up.

The important thing is both of you should be in it to win it, not just one of you. Every couple I interviewed stated this. "We knew we had to be in it for the long haul," is what they often said. I agree. They meant they had to both be committed to the business, and both find passion in it.

4 Ways to Keep the Fire Going in Your Commitment as a Couple:

- **Take a quarterly personal retreat**

- **Sign up for a goal assessment class at the end or beginning of every year to assess how far you have come and where you want to go**

- **Be encouraging to each other—keep a positive attitude**

- **List your goals somewhere in your office so you can both see them**

Think about it as the two of you establish your little corner of the earth. It's something you have made from scratch, built from nothing except your heart and soul, and you want to share it with others. If the drive and passion for what you two have decided to do is not there, don't even attempt this. Being in it to win it is exactly that: both of you contributing all of your heart and soul and determination to succeed, and in all aspects of both your marriage and your business. Nothing less.

So what happens when one of you is not "in it to win it?" How do you conquer that hurdle? I, myself, have run into this. My husband has taken on ventures that I was not crazy about. Even though I wanted to help him succeed, I grew more resentful for being pushed into something I did not want to do. I'd finally had enough one day and confronted him with my feelings. He had no idea I hated what we were doing that much. We quickly put a plan in place to phase me out of that aspect of the business. I was much happier after that, although I kicked myself for taking so long to talk with him about it.

The thing to remember here is to communicate about what the two of you are "in it to win it" *for*. What is your mutually agreed-on goal? One reason I was hesitant to speak with my husband about the thing I hated was because I also wanted to be respectful of his wish to keep dealing with it. I knew I did not want to be a part of it, but I knew he would want to remain involved in it and I had to adjust to that. So it is with you. It all goes back to compromise. It is very possible that one or both of you will not always have the "in it to win it" mentality about all aspects of your business. My best advice is to constantly be on top of the situation before it escalates into something ugly.

Meet the Slaughters

Mark and Pat Slaughter are the epitome of being in it to win it. When I interviewed them, most of the stories they told me revolved around their passion and drive for what they do.

Since they met, they have created a life around fitness, health and wellness. They absolutely love it. Even though they had been running a successful fitness business since they got married, they'd recently added physical therapy to their mix of services when I spoke with them. From the beginning, Mark and Pat knew (from what they'd seen in others and what they'd each learned about themselves when they worked for other people) that both of them being 100 percent dedicated was critical to their success.

They must be, because they have been working together for twenty-eight years and counting, and married for even longer.

Mark and Pat got married when Pat was still working at another job. Soon, however, she started helping Mark run a fitness club where he was a manager. He then became owner and together they grew the business so big they were ready to move on to the ultimate goal—their own physical therapy center. By this time, they knew their passion for fitness and well-being was sustainable and mutual. Consequently, they sold the fitness club so Mark could attend physical therapy school to pursue their dream.

After graduating, they opened their own office with the same pride and determination they had when they ran the fitness studio. "You have to be willing to study and to learn what you don't know. You have to be willing to not only run your business, but to constantly be improving it and yourself," says Mark. Love what you do and do it with everything you have in you.

Pat spent her time capitalizing on her strengths—setting up processes for interacting with patients on a non-medical level, for example. She created not only a front office, but its accompanying paperwork, policies and procedures. Most importantly, she figured out how to get paid from insurance companies, which they had not dealt with at the fitness club.

"You make a lot of mistakes, but that is how you learn," says Pat. Perseverance and determination is what it takes. Of course, the drive to want to pay your mortgage and eat doesn't hurt either! Now she finds it hard to have even a part-time assistant; she feels like she's handing over her baby for someone else to take care of!

Pat and Mark often bring the workday home with them and talk about their business when they're away from it. "You can't help it," they say. Thinking about the business and constantly wanting to improve it—and themselves, in terms of how they run it together—just comes with the territory. They may have disagreed during the day about certain things, and they may still not agree on it by evening, but in the end, they always respect the person who made the final decision and, thus, compromise is born. In the beginning, they caution, this can be an everyday occurrence!

Another important recommendation they made is to communicate regularly about the business, yet also to respect the other person's need to take a break from talking about it. Rome was not built in a day. Learn to watch your spouse's behavior and know that tomorrow is another day and you can take care of it then, together.

They also recommend learning to respect the other person's strengths when you don't agree on how to accomplish something in the office. "Pat always wants to lovingly put in her two cents' worth with me on a patient's status, but she ultimately defers to my judgment," Mark says. He defers to hers when it comes to running the office, he added. They have learned to compromise when they don't agree. They decided long ago the person in charge of a particular area of the business will need to make the final decision, .

They've clearly learned to work it out when they don't agree, and they're also excellent at trusting the other one.

Mark's secret to their success is all about compromise: "Let her do what she wants and you do what she wants."

Good advice and well said, Mark! The perfect example of compromise! Just kidding ... sort of ...

Soul-Searching Questions

What is your business going to provide? What need does your business fulfill? More importantly, what are you passionate about? If you are not all that passionate about the type of business you and your spouse are considering, can you see yourself devoting 100 percent of your time to working with your spouse on the business?

_____

_____

_____

_____

_____

_____

_____

_____

_____

_____

Is your relationship strong enough to handle spending a lot of time together? Do you vacation well together, for example?

_____

_____

_____

_____

_____

_____

_____

_____

_____

_____

_____

_____

Can you compromise with your spouse? Are you willing to admit when you are wrong? What about your spouse—can he or she do the same?

_____

_____

_____

_____

_____

_____

_____

_____

_____

_____

_____

Do you both have the right mindset to handle the stress and pressure that comes with business ownership? For example, do you panic when you do not know what to do? Do you push blame or find a solution? What do you each do when you're stressed, and can you each handle the other one's reaction to stress?

_____

_____

_____

_____

_____

_____

_____

_____

_____

_____

Can you respect each other's strengths and weaknesses and work together to maximize each other's potential? Are you willing to take a step back when the decision to be made is not in your area of strength?

_____

_____

_____

_____

_____

_____

_____

_____

_____

_____

What large problem have you had to deal with already as a couple, and what process did you use to reach a solution? Did the process pretty much work for both of you? How would (or did) you refine it for future use? For example, how did you deal—as a couple—with a parent's declining health and the issues around that, or the loss of a job, or particularly trying times with a teenager, or blending your ready-made families if one or both of you have children from a previous relationship?

_____

_____

_____

_____

_____

_____

_____

_____

_____

Chapter
Two

Let her do what she wants.

Then, do what she wants you to do.

After that, everyone will be happy.

Mark Slaughter,
co-owner of Fitness 4 Life Physical Therapy

Divide and Conquer

Who Is in Charge?

Each couple I interviewed urged prospective husband-and-wife teams to discuss the "who is in charge" question immediately. The answer contains the most valuable information you'll each give and receive. Face the division-of-labor issue head on!

Don't wait. Otherwise, you might fall into the trap of "I will take care of it myself," and you'll be in trouble—quickly. Taking on too many duties leads to resentment and arguments about who is doing more. The situation will soon spiral out of control.

Define your roles in the company from day one. Who is in charge of sales? Who does the marketing? Who pays the bills? Who answers the phone? Who schedules the appointments? Address and agree on all of these before you open the door of your business, or as you encounter new tasks. Deal with them right away. Remember, both of you need to buy into these decisions, so make sure you are in agreement.

How do you begin to define roles? Start with the obvious. Whichever person has the specific skill on which the business is based, choose that person to get the work done or to act as the primary salesperson. Here's an example. You and your husband are purchasing an automotive repair company. He's the expert under the hood—you don't even know how to open the hood! Put him in charge of repairing the vehicles in your company's shop, or have him oversee employees' work while he also serves as the head salesman. In this scenario, you'd likely be tapped for administrative duties, and the two of you could divide the rest.

Don't let tradition or stereotypes stand in the way of efficiency and logic. If one of you is chatty and personable, that person should focus on the customers or handle sales efforts requiring face time with prospects. If one of you is better with numbers, guess who is assigned the bookkeeping duties? Whoever is stronger at one particular task should be the one in charge of it, no matter what tradition suggests.

Decide who's the boss. If you are both strong-willed and want to be in charge, this can be a sensitive issue. Think about it. Who would be best at this position? Is it the person on whose skills the business is based? Is it the person in the manager's role? Is it the person with the most management experience?

I saw how the wrong decision can impact a business—and how the right one can fix it—when I worked for a doctor. Wonderful guy, but a terrible boss. The business was obviously based on his skills, but he was very laid back and wanted to be friends with everyone. Consequently, no one followed through when he assigned a duty or task. He did not have enough authority once he became too much of a friend to his employees. The boss's role quickly fell to his wife. Once that was established, it was a much happier environment. People did as she asked, so the office ran smoothly and everyone still loved and respected the doctor.

I recommend making a list of what needs to be done, then discuss the list, one item at a time. Don't overload one person with too many tasks. That's why a list is helpful. Putting it on paper helps you see the division of labor and where you might need to tweak it. Arrange the information in a flow chart if necessary. Showing the information visually and using colors often helps.

Divide and Conquer List

	Husband	Wife	Outsource
Accounting/bill-paying/bill-collecting/ payroll	☐	☐	☐
Marketing (networking events, special events, advertising decisions)	☐	☐	☐
Sales	☐	☐	☐
Employee relations/human resources	☐	☐	☐
Customer service	☐	☐	☐
Answering the phone	☐	☐	☐
Inventory management/dealing with vendors	☐	☐	☐
Scheduling appointments	☐	☐	☐
Maintenance/upkeep of storefront or other work areas	☐	☐	☐

Your business has tasks that are specific to what you do. Add those tasks here and determine who they belong to.

Now that you have a list, develop a plan of action to avoid confusion and tripping over each other. Without a plan detailing all aspects of your division of labor, chaos reigns. Nothing gets accomplished. So write your list, fill in your plan and respect the decisions you made.

Try it for a month. You'll see where you need adjustments, or if all facets are working well. Do not be afraid to reevaluate quickly if necessary.

Follow up these decisions with actions that support them. For instance, a management meeting on the same day every week ensures everyone is on the same page, even if it is just the two of you. It is easy to get caught up in the day's events and forget to tell your spouse about a new shipment that arrived, for example, or a phone call from the CPA.

Remain organized by holding regular staff meetings. I noticed how critical this is in my own business, and I heard it from all the couples. Our advice to you: Reserve time at the office or even in the evening to discuss or review whatever needs addressing or communicating. You don't need to go all "corporate" or anything like that. Make your meetings fun! Hold them almost anywhere. The point is to have them.

Regular staff meetings position you to more easily discover, assess and fix a problem. You can also celebrate what is going right and expand on those successes. My husband and I used to have Friday morning meetings. Invariably, we skipped a few, then a few more, and chaos soon erupted. Then we'd get our act together, start holding our meetings again and everything would run more smoothly ... until we started slacking off again. Hey, we're human too! But we now clearly see the need for the meetings. They help you stay on top of what needs to be accomplished, what isn't working and what is succeeding brilliantly. Try bringing doughnuts to your meeting. They always made ours more palatable!

Capitalize on Your Sphere of Influence

Don't underestimate the power of whom you know. If you're the one with great connections to attorneys, then all legal matters should be your responsibility. You may not be an expert on the subject, but you know people who are. If you have influence in these areas, it will really help.

Form relationships of trust. Brain trusts, mastermind groups, networking groups—whatever it takes. These relationships will not only help you accomplish your tasks, but they'll also provide accountability. Choose to take on tasks when you have people in your corner who've got your back. Duties are often delegated to the person who knows someone who can help. Spend time forming relationships of trust.

Below, write the name of each person you're assigning to a role featured on the list. These are your people—the ones you'll turn to when you need help in their areas of expertise. They are your brain trust, your worthy advisors.

The Brain Trust List

  Banker

  Accountant

  Attorney

  Technology expert/consultant

  Financial advisor

  Insurance provider

  Marketing consultant

  Massage therapist

  Business coach

  Other business owners you trust

Be sure to add people to this list whose advice is pertinent to your business.

Remember, Patience ... Patience!

When you are at work, treat each other with respect, especially in front of the employees. Just because you know your spouse will forgive you when you're a jerk doesn't mean you should behave like one. Respect each other's strengths and act accordingly. The couples I interviewed all said they are often less patient, less understanding and less tolerant of mistakes made by each other than they are with their employees. Even though this is human nature, it will damage your entire relationship if you let it get out of control.

One couple in particular comes to mind. He screamed at his wife in front of his employees, which was extremely demeaning. The situation was uncomfortable for everyone, including the employees. The couple finally solved this issue by sitting down and really talking about how these situations felt. After coming up with a plan, they worked hard to avoid the triggers and to change their negative reactions to unavoidably stressful situations. Both the couple and the employees are now working much better together.

It is imperative you treat your spouse with the same respect you do anyone else in the workplace. Save your rants for behind closed doors or later, when you're away from the business, customers and employees.

"What We Have Here Is a Failure to Communicate ..."

Don't let this happen to you. I know you have heard this time and time again: communication is key. For entrepreneurs, however, it is essential. I believe successful entrepreneurial couples possess incredible communication skills. They must! When you're running a business, there is no time to play games with each other or develop an attitude or have a pity party.

As we've mentioned, effective communication also means compromise. Acquiesce gracefully, and pick your battles carefully. Another sign you're communicating well is knowing you can communicate anything to the other person and not be punished for how you feel. Being able to comfortably explain how you feel about something opens the door to finding solutions to the problem.

On the other hand, how can you expect your spouse to communicate with you if you are just going to rip their head off when they express a concern? Something to think about, isn't it?

What if Neither of You Knows How to Do Something?

Just because there are two of you, and you are both incredibly smart people, doesn't mean you can do everything. Couples who work together don't outsource as much as business professionals who don't work with their spouses. I know it feels like you can save money when your spouse is capable of undertaking an out-of-the-ordinary task, but think of the time saved when you hire an expert!

I cannot tell you how many times I tried to deal with things myself and ended up wasting time and money. Worse, I never accomplished the goal. Or else I did it completely wrong in the end anyway. I should have hired an expert.

Many people say, "But I cannot afford to hire someone."

To that, I respond, "Can you afford not to?"

How much is your time really worth? For example, is it a good and efficient use of time to spend several hours dealing with your failing computer when, instead, you could have hired an expert and moved on to an income-generating task? A lot of people get caught up in believing they don't have the money. I am telling you right now, you do. I am convinced your time is better spent working on something that will bring in money.

Let's do some math to prove my advice is financially sound. We'll assume you charge $100 an hour for your services. Your computer goes down and you spend four hours troubleshooting, implementing your chosen solution, and getting everything put back to where you were to begin with. You just spent the equivalent of $400 working on something that an expert could fix in one hour at the same rate, give or take. Meanwhile, you could have been finishing other jobs, returning phone calls, closing a deal on a new job—everything you put on hold for four hours while you tried to fix your computer. Keep in mind, too, that many professional services do not cost as much as you think they do.

It can be scary and intimidating to call for help. Society has trained us to be a do-it-yourself society. In the business world, that can get you into trouble. If you are not an expert, and don't have time to become one, hire someone who is. Stop delegating to your spouse just because that is what you are used to doing or because she's the only other employee.

6 Things to Delegate to Someone Other Than Your Spouse

1. **Accounting—unless you are an accountant, this takes too much time to do on your own.**

2. **Anything legal—don't download your own legal forms and play at being an attorney, because you'll regret it.**

3. **Technology—unless you know exactly what you are doing, hire an expert to save time and aggravation.**

4. **Marketing/PR—this is a big job that can be divided and delegated. It also helps to have fresh, unbiased ideas coming in the door. This should also include advertising, and your website and blog, for example.**

5. **Office tasks—filing, follow-up calls to confirm appointments, etc.**

6. Home/office cleaning—how many appointments can you go on or projects can you finish in the time it takes to clean your home, office or storefront?

In conclusion, decide to not waste your time or your spouse's by dealing with something you could outsource. Use your spouse's strengths to have him or her work on something that will make your business more profitable. Call an expert to handle those tasks you are not good at or really don't want to do. Form relationships with these experts and you'll soon have a hand-picked (or personally referred) group of experts at your fingertips. Just remember, don't be afraid to delegate.

Who Is Doing the Dishes Tonight?

Now that we've discussed who is handling what at the office, we can discuss the home front.

Uh oh, forgot about that.

That was the response from most of the husbands I interviewed. I even had one who simply stated, "I have people for that." If that is the case, great. But who is ultimately in charge of the tasks around the house? The cooking, cleaning, grocery shopping, laundry, yard work, home maintenance, and so on. If those roles are not clearly defined, you will have just as much chaos at home as you will at the office—especially if home and office are located in the same place.

This topic clearly struck a nerve with the couples I interviewed. Their responses ranged from laughter to scowls to sighs, although I did receive a few happy responses. One couple half-jokingly recommended getting a prenuptial agreement.

Sometimes, if you have already dealt with these duties before your business started, this is a non-issue. But for those of you who struggled from the beginning, throwing a business into the mix will only make household jobs more complicated.

So, again, look at the division of labor. Share the responsibilities the same way. Have clearly defined roles of who can do what. Split them up. If one of you is taking on most of the housework and working full-time at the office, there will be problems, I can assure you. Go back to the list and verify you are equally sharing the duties. Establishing clearly defined roles from the beginning will definitely head fights off at the pass.

When all else fails, rock-paper-scissors works every time. You laugh, but I often do this. It works. Don't knock it. Respect it, and the decisions that arise from it.

Household Assignments List

	Husband	Wife	Kids	Other
Cleaning	☐	☐	☐	☐
Cooking	☐	☐	☐	☐
Grocery shopping	☐	☐	☐	☐
Laundry	☐	☐	☐	☐
Shuttling kids to/from school	☐	☐	☐	☐
Assisting with homework	☐	☐	☐	☐
Pet care	☐	☐	☐	☐
Outdoor maintenance	☐	☐	☐	☐
Home repairs	☐	☐	☐	☐
Trash detail	☐	☐	☐	☐

List any other activity that is unique to your family and who is in charge of handling it.

Meet the Bridgemans

With eleven years' experience operating their insurance brokerage company, Andy and Kathy Bridgeman now handle every kind of insurance you can imagine. Before they started their own company, however, Andy worked for another insurance firm. Kathy attended school part-time to become a teacher and focused the rest of her time on raising their kids. Going into business with her husband was a big change for her.

The Bridgemans explained how, in the beginning, Andy's expectations were "amped up," or way too high. Because he had previous experience in the insurance industry, he felt he knew what needed to be done and was eager to make his own business successful. Unfortunately, his gung-ho enthusiasm got in the way of careful planning.

Andy and Kathy struggled the first two years and primarily about who was in charge. Duties were never established; they were left up in the air. The couple based decisions on what caused the least amount of harm. Their lack of communication impacted their finances the most. One-half of the couple would make a money-related decision and then act on it, but not communicate it to the other. Overlapping efforts became a real problem. Anger and anxiety spilled over into all aspects of the business and continued at home.

Eventually, they realized what was happening. Once they established their roles and greatly improved their communication, this eliminated their overlapping efforts. To accomplish this, they sat down and—over the course of several meetings—decided whose skill set would better suit each job. They were honest with themselves about who that would be.

As they made their list, they saw a pattern, which helped them to make decisions on new tasks later on. Their plan evolved as tasks changed hands a few times based on altered circumstances, but at least they had a good direction.

Today, their firm is flourishing and so is their marriage. Andy and Kathy recommend understanding the roles of each person in the business, and giving that person the space and respect to get the job done.

And when all else fails, rock-paper-scissors!

Soul-Searching Questions

Who is in charge of sales? Do either you or your spouse have any experience with sales? Do either of you enjoy making sales calls or visits? Do either of you like to talk with people in person?

_____

_____

_____

_____

_____

_____

_____

_____

_____

_____

_____

Who does the marketing? Do either of you have any experience with marketing or sales promotion or advertising? What about your website—does one of you enjoy working with online tools and applications to develop and/or maintain your company's site?

_____

_____

_____

_____

_____

_____

_____

_____

_____

_____

_____

Who pays the bills? Do either of you have any accounting or bookkeeping experience? Is one of you good with numbers or more analytical than the other? How do you currently manage responsibility for household bills?

_____

_____

_____

_____

_____

_____

_____

_____

_____

_____

Who answers the phone? Are either of you good (i.e., professional, responsive, available) with phone calls? Do you enjoy talking to people on the phone?

_____

_____

_____

_____

_____

_____

_____

_____

_____

_____

_____

_____

_____

Who schedules the appointments? Does it make sense for one of you to manage the other's schedule? Will this allow the other person to spend more time on profitable tasks?

_____

_____

_____

_____

_____

_____

_____

_____

_____

_____

_____

_____

Who will take on the manager role? Is one of you a natural leader? Do either of you work well under direction?

_____

_____

_____

_____

_____

_____

_____

_____

_____

_____

_____

_____

How are household tasks currently managed and/or delegated?
Chores, kids, shopping, for instance?

_____

_____

_____

_____

_____

_____

_____

_____

_____

_____

_____

_____

Chapter
Three

Don't let people drive you crazy when you know it is within walking distance.

Unknown author

The Snowball of Crabbiness

Perhaps the most critical factor in running a business with your spouse is how well you can each handle stress. Let's face it; marriage alone can be stressful enough. Throw in running a business and you will find out just how strong your relationship is. The good news is that with the right mindset, you can channel stress as a tool to build a stronger relationship. We'll discuss how to do that in this chapter. And, yes, it's worthy of its own chapter.

The Crabby Virus

The ugly truth is that crabbiness is like a virus—it will spread quickly. It is human nature to return crabby with crabby. Lash out at your spouse and they will likely lash back. The crabbiness will spread to those around you. People who are around other crabby people usually behave more negatively. At the very least, it creates an uncomfortable environment—at worst, it becomes a full-blown snowball of crabbiness.

But measures can be taken to contain the virus. Just like you take certain measures to not contract a flu virus, you too, can take steps to not fall into the crabbiness trap.

Establishing a Filter

Let's start with a common example. You are in the middle of a bad day and you become snappy with or lash out at your spouse. We have all had similar situations. And, like most people, you would never dream of treating an acquaintance like that, let alone a friend or fellow employee. Yet it's easy to dump on the people we love. We know they'll love us, despite our crabby attitude. We also become comfortable with the people we are around the most often or feel closest to, so we tend to speak more impulsively or not think about our words or actions before expressing ourselves.

When we're around people we don't know well, most of us have a filter that we use to screen our words and attitude. The more we get to know someone, the more the filter wears away or we don't feel the need to use it. We speak more freely and allow more of our emotions to show. We use the filter less and less.

If you've been with your spouse a long time, that filter may be completely gone. This is where most couples make one of their biggest mistakes.

In marriage, especially if you're running a business together, you need that filter. That filter may be the only thing standing between your crabbiness and your ability—as a couple—to work out the issue. My couples pointed out a good rule of thumb: treat each other like co-workers while you are in the office. Most of us would never talk to another co-worker in a nasty or inflammatory tone. We'd handle it in a more professional manner. Just because you are married to a co-worker does not give you the right to snap at your spouse if you are having a bad day.

5 Tips to Better Filter Communications with Your Spouse:

1. **Think before you speak.**

2. **Mind your manners and be polite—just like you would with anyone else.**

3. **Choose to finish the conversation later, when you have had time to think it through more clearly and, hopefully, less emotionally.**

4. **Choose your words carefully, and don't be accusatory or nasty.**

5. Be patient and allow the other person to finish before you respond.

Nip It in the Bud

One idea is to be the bigger person and head the makings of a bad situation off at the pass. It sounds like such a simple thing to do, and it can be, but many couples just cannot nip their crabbiness in the bud. It's tough to do—I know—especially if you've just arrived at the office, for example, and things are already insanely busy. Before you know it, you are overwhelmed with escalating stress, so the crabby factor rears its ugly head. But either you or your spouse must have the clearer head and take a step back to settle things down.

Crabbiness and fighting can be avoided if you just don't allow things to escalate in the first place. Controlling your feelings before they escalate into a behavior that is completely unnecessary and unproductive is something that, ideally, should be practiced from the beginning of a relationship, not just when starting a business.

One method I use to nip it in the bud is to think of this negative behavior as one I don't want my child to see. If you're a parent, you've worked to control your child's behavior, and hopefully you've done your best to manage your own unruly or unwanted behaviors to set a good example for them. The same thing should happen when you work with your spouse and run a business together: Don't let crabbiness take over and rule the day. Check your attitude at the door and your day will be pleasant. You could even pretend your child is there, watching how mom and dad interact when they have a difference of opinion or something stressful is happening.

Laser Focus

When problems arise, couples must have a laser focus on fixing the issues, rather than fighting with each other. This means focusing only on the specific situation to get at what is at the heart of these negative feelings. By blocking out the crabbiness, everyone can move on, potentially eliminating the problems that bring on the crabby in the first place. We all know that fighting does not lead to solutions, that it's a waste of time, and it is hurtful. It does not yield the desired results, and it diverts attention to something much less important than growing and running your business.

Obviously, no one is perfect, and crabbiness and fighting will occasionally win out. Then what? If you find yourself getting angry at your spouse, consider why you are really upset in the first place. Oftentimes there is an underlying reason to a specific argument. It may not be what you are actually arguing about and, instead, you're upset about something completely different that hasn't even been mentioned yet. If you take time to get to the root of the actual problem and address a way to fix it, your crabby factor will decrease dramatically.

Grudge-holding has no place in a business environment. Arguments often erupt because one person is angry about something that happened previously. What would happen if you actually talked about that, instead of the current topic that pushed you over the edge and into the abyss of crabbiness? Maybe the other person will get mad, but I guarantee you will feel better if you just deal with it head on. The root of the disagreement has to be solved before you move ahead, otherwise, the snowball just keeps getting bigger and bigger.

This is where that old saying, never go to bed angry, comes into play. A lot of couples say they don't necessarily follow this rule, but it is important to consider and strive for it. Harboring feelings for more than a day, instead of using that laser focus I mentioned earlier, only leads to tension and confusion. Get to the root of it and fix it. Doing so often means you can more easily control your emotions and focus on the smaller issue at hand.

5 Ways to Help You Get Control of a Crabby Situation:

1. **Take a time out. Walk away to have a cooler head. Get a massage while you are gone. It will help!**

2. Try yoga or some other exercise to learn how to manage stress.

3. Stand on one foot for one minute. The concentration that is required to accomplish this will help dissolve your crabbiness.

4. Take a shower. A lot of people do their best thinking in the shower, and warm water is relaxing!

5. Keep things in perspective. Make a list of what is really important. Share it with your spouse.

Know When to Hold 'Em and ...

Know when to walk away. Sometimes, you just need to agree to disagree. There will be plenty of times when one or both of you will think your way is the best and the other will not budge. It is okay. You are both human. You will not always agree. You may both have different ideas about how to run the business, deal with employees, allocate funds, whatever it is. The important thing is to respect the final decision in the end. Disagreements are going to happen, but deal with them in a way that is respectful to your spouse.

Many couples suggest leaving the argument for a while. As I mentioned in the list above, take a walk or go for a drive, and get away from the situation to clear your head. Remove yourself from the building or the presence of your spouse. Sometimes, if you just step away, the solution will present itself. Or you might see that your way may not be the best way. Or you'll decide it's okay to not reach a decision until after you've discussed it further, at a later date.

One couple pointed out the importance of having separate lunches. Sometimes the lunches would be with other people, sometimes just by themselves, but they often came back refreshed, calmed down and ready to deal with whatever situation had been a problem earlier in the day.

The main thing is to just lay your hand down before you lose all your chips. It is about cooperation, not coercion. Do what is best for the business by moving on. Some people who have been working with their spouses for a long time admitted to having ego problems in the beginning, and I notice this a lot with younger couples. Could it be that the couples who have done this longer have learned from their own mistakes that egos just waste time?

Another particularly helpful suggestion was to write about it. Several of the wives, in particular, said they would write a letter to their husband, venting all of their grief and frustration, call him names, yell and scream, and then throw the letter away. Just the act of getting it down on paper made them feel better. By the time they were done with the letter, they were less angry and felt a little better. Seeing their anger in print also made them calm down. When they read it, they thought, "Wow, this is mean!" and then threw it away or shredded it so it wouldn't make them mad again if they came across it later.

Others kept a journal of disagreements, for the same reason: it made them feel better to write down their frustrations down. They made sure to keep the journal in a safe place, however, away from their spouse. When another disagreement occurs, the journal writers explained, they go back to their journals, skim previous entries and laugh at those arguments, wondering why in the world they were so mad at their spouses. Occasionally, what they read only further proves their point about how smart they are!

Another person suggested using earphones. The mere act of plugging into a computer or iPod and listening to a personalized playlist allows a person to mentally and emotionally escape and clear his or her head. Since clearer heads always prevail, you should do whatever you have to do to make sure you are the one with the clearer head. That might mean creating a playlist just for times when you're wound up, frustrated or stressed out. Music is powerful, and there is no reason you can't use it to help you in tense situations. Just make sure you're not rude about retreating to your own world that, in effect, shuts out other people and noises (such as a ringing telephone, if you're on phone duty).

Containing the Virus

Another important thing to remember is to be unified in front of your employees. Do not let them see there is a division between the two of you, or they may treat you like some children treat their parents: they'll go ask mom when dad says no. That is the last thing you want going on in your office. It is easy for employees to see which person has which side of the argument when you fight in front of them. This will only give them ammunition and you the feeling of being ganged up on by your spouse and your employees. If the employees side with you, your spouse might feel attacked from all fronts, and that's not conducive to bringing him or her around to your way of thinking.

Remember, this business is something you created together, just like you did your kids. Don't allow what you created to take over and run the show; you don't allow your kids to run your household, so don't allow your employees to run your company.

A Spoonful of Sugar

In the movie Mary Poppins, there is a scene in which young Jane and Michael do not want to clean their room. Mary Poppins, their nanny, says, "In every job that must be done, there is an element of fun. Find the fun and—snap—the job's a game!" Just like Mary, you can also relieve crabbiness and stress by making those times more playful. Consider how to add play or humor to the situation and alleviate whatever it is you are arguing about. Make it into a game if you need to. Tell jokes around it, come up with creative text messages to get your point across—whatever you can think of.

When I was writing this book, I have to admit I got very irritable around the house at times. To alleviate my crankiness before it snowballed out of control, my husband pointed out all the pearls of wisdom in my own book. He would mention one and then say, "I read that somewhere." It was both funny and helpful to be reminded of my own ideas, and it helped improve my mood. I'd learned by then that humor can be extremely helpful when we're both receptive to it. It goes a long way toward defusing tense situations.

In the earlier days of our marriage and business partnership, however, I was unreceptive to the humor. Some people do not respond well to humor in tense situations, and I still have to work at it occasionally.

No matter how well or poorly the cranky person responds, humor must be used appropriately, and it cannot be a substitute for action. Above all, know what your spouse can and cannot handle, in order to be the most supportive.

Humor works best when a solution is being proposed, when you're trying to change a train of thought, or to allow time for creative thinking. Back to when I was writing and cranky: my husband was trying to make me laugh so my creative mind could get going again and I could keep working. When I allowed the humor in, I laughed and had no reason to be crabby with him.

When you and your spouse disagree about a business decision and one or both of you is cranky, I suggest making it into a game. Here's an example: One couple agreed that they would each try things the other person's way for one week and evaluate what happened during that time. Whichever person's idea benefitted the business more would prevail. They set very specific ground rules as to what they felt "benefit the business" meant in each circumstance, and off they went. Thus, they had a game with rules and a winner, but, first and foremost, it was a game. They successfully injected an element of fun into the situation, and this strategy worked really well for them. They streamlined some aspects of their business that needed attention, and now they apply it to problems all the time.

Why not try simple acts of kindness for your spouse to help improve everyone's attitude and avoid the snowball of crabbiness? Running an errand on his behalf, or bringing her a drink when she's really busy are great ideas. So is sending a quick e-card or something fun to his email, just to keep him on his toes.

Random acts of kindness, mixed with a positive attitude, will always help.

"A" Is for Attitude

One of this word's definitions is how you choose to deal with what life hands you. You can choose to be stressed or calm. You can choose how to deal with your spouse. You can be crabby or you can put that person on a pedestal. You make the choice every day—every hour or minute of every day, for that matter.

Try to keep it all in perspective. Is a particular problem really all that bad that you must attack your spouse over it? Will the results of your actions cause greater problems than what you are crabby about in the first place?

The only person who can make stressful times more stressful is you. So choose your attitude and know that you're in control of how you think and feel about the situation.

Meet the DeLassuses—Chiropractic Care Providers

Dr. Barry and Melissa DeLassus have been married for two years. They own and operate a chiropractic office, which they opened together. According to Melissa, she was the one who had to make more changes, because Barry had known for years— well before they met—that he wanted to have his own practice.

When they talked about starting the business and combining their skills, Melissa knew she would need to embrace the roles of entrepreneur and idea person—both of which she has grown to love.

Barry and Melissa shared with me that they now feel they talked about work too much when they first started their business. They realized they were focusing too much on the business and not enough on each other, which resulted in some cranky times. When they focused on getting to the root of the problem, they found their relationship improved if they took time to pursue their separate interests. Having a life outside of the office was very helpful in combating those cranky moments. Not being around each other all the time made them appreciate even more what they had as a couple, which led to fewer arguments.

They also recommended leaving personal issues at home. "It was very important to both of us that, no matter what, patients have no idea that any issues might be going on at home. Patients will definitely pick up on our irritability, so it was imperative that we not bring this into the office with us," Barry explained.

Melissa mentioned that the same rule applies in terms of not arguing in front of their employees. As we discussed earlier in this chapter, creating a happy work environment from the top down, and setting a good example in front of employees, is the right way to go. No need to bring them into it, or pit them against one of you.

Melissa also suggested making stressful times cheerful and doing something else to get your mind off of the negatives. "By simply adding a little humor to the situation, our disagreements suddenly seemed smaller and easier to tackle." Diverging down a humorous path, even for a minute, means they're taking time away from their arguments, and they can return to the conversation from a place of being better able to evaluate what they had been discussing, and learn from it. When Melissa gets stressed, Barry pokes fun at Melissa's crazy schedule, just like my husband does with my crabbiness when I'm writing. Humor diffuses so much stress. Try it!

The couple pointed out that the relationship should always come first. The business may go away or other circumstances in their lives may change, but the marriage is the foundation that everything is based on. They created it together, so they can and should deal with the stressful times together, too. Those tough moments are just a minute part of running a business and staying married. It is how you handle them—with your attitude and your determination to make running your business together worthwhile—that makes you successful. Melissa and Barry say they have learned so much from each other since the beginning of not only their marriage, but working together too. Above all, they are having fun—and succeeding.

If you are still crabby, however, there is always chapter four ...

Soul-Searching Questions

Does something happen on a regular basis in your business that stresses you out? Why is it stressing you out? Is it something your spouse can handle, instead of you?

_____

_____

_____

_____

_____

_____

_____

_____

_____

_____

_____

_____

What types of activities help you to relieve stress? List three things you can do to calm down.

_____

_____

_____

_____

_____

_____

_____

_____

_____

_____

_____

_____

Why are you really upset? What action or circumstance created the reason for you to be upset?

_____

_____

_____

_____

_____

_____

_____

_____

_____

_____

_____

_____

Have you ever gone to bed angry over something that pertained only to your business? Did holding on to that anger really accomplish anything? How did you resolve it the next day?

What if you got it off your chest, but privately? Try writing why you are mad in a letter, or make a list of your frustrations to clear your head.

_____

_____

_____

_____

_____

_____

_____

_____

_____

_____

_____

_____

What simple acts of kindness can you do to lighten a tense situation? List at least four.

_____

_____

_____

_____

_____

_____

_____

_____

_____

_____

_____

_____

Chapter
Four

Don't wear flannel.
Victoria's Secret needs to be part of
every family-owned business!

Jules Karagiannis, owner of The Tenderloin Room

From Boardroom to Bedroom

Be Like Nike—*Just Do It*

One of the hardest issues for couples who work together is sex and intimacy. That is, how to deal with both the boardroom and the bedroom.

It's not always easy. The two of you work together all day long in a professional capacity, and then, suddenly, at home, you are not supposed to be co-workers any more. You're now spouses, with a completely different set of rules and expectations. And, the next morning, it starts all over again, but in the reverse order.

Sex is important to married life, but it can definitely get more complicated when you work together.

"Oh, my God, don't even think about touching me after what you did today!" This was a statement I heard more than once when I talked with people about this topic. Is it wrong to feel that way? No. Those feelings are completely understandable and common. And they're not the end of the world—or the marriage.

Not surprisingly, sex was a particularly sensitive subject in all my interviews with couples. Many of the couples said it is a constant concern—one that takes focus and care to overcome, but that it's worth it. Just like in any marriage.

Dispensing advice on how to maintain your sex life is a difficult thing. Everyone handles it differently, and no one is an expert on your boardroom-to-bedroom situation except you. After all, you two are the only ones who know what goes on in there.

So, how do you handle it? How do you find the balance between your dual roles of co-worker and spouse?

The solution is the same as it's always been—make intimacy a priority. Humans need it, and it's vital to the health of your marriage. Don't put sex and physical intimacy on the back burner, because it only leads to trouble, anger and resentment.

Remember, the two of you are married for a reason. You love, respect and are attracted to that person, and you obviously want to spend the rest of your life with him or her. So, the quick and dirty answer to this concern lies in this section's subtitle, "just do it."

As you navigate from boardroom to bedroom, here are things to consider.

Find New Ways to Talk about Your Day

When you both arrive home after work, you are now in spouse mode. Gone, however, is the age-old question, "Honey, how was your day?" You typically already know the answer!

So, what do you say? How do you reconnect in spouse mode with each other?

Every couple in business together faces this question. In the beginning, you might feel frustrated and that you can't tell your spouse about your day—he or she was likely there and probably knows all about it.

Here's a tip: Try talking about it from a different angle. You can openly share—now that you're away from employees and customers—how you felt about a particular situation. You've also had a bit of time and distance to gain new perspective. Put a different spin on things so you can still discuss your day.

Bad Days Put the Fire Out and
Good Days Fuel the Fire

Let's be clear on this point: Just because you are running a business together does not mean you need to be super humans. You are just like any other married couple at the end of the day. If you had a bad day, you will probably not feel especially romantic toward your spouse. Meetings go awry, and employees or customers frustrate you. Financial issues inevitably crop up that keep you awake at night, so your patience is short-lived or you're snippy and cranky. Or one of you may drop the ball and the consequences land on the other person's plate. The last thing you want is to go home and have sex with the very person whose mess you spent the whole day cleaning up. Sound familiar?

This particular issue will probably come up more often in the beginning, when you're still establishing roles and duties and getting things off the ground. At some point, you'll realize, *Oh, no—I have to go home and be loving and sweet. Crap! I don't even like you right now!*

Don't fall into the trap of thinking you'll get around to intimacy later, or some other day. If it would have been normal to be intimate that night (and especially if you'd planned it), don't let the bad day stop you. A bad day is a fact of life, so set it aside. Go home, and remember: tomorrow is another day. Whatever is bothering you will wait, you can be sure of that.

When you do have a good day, everything is better. You landed that account, got that check in the mail you've been waiting for, accomplished a sales goal, or solved a tough problem you've been working on. Whatever the case may be, take advantage of these situations. When you are in a good mood, or you are up to date with work tasks, for example, take time to appreciate each other. Happy days mean happy nights. You married this person for a reason—now is the time to revel in that decision. Enjoy each other's company in whatever way you can. Good days can sometimes seem few and far between. So, go ahead—pounce!

Take Advantage of When, Where and How

Think about it. You are with that person all day. You actually have more opportunities to squeeze in time together than other couples do. I am not suggesting you neglect deadlines, but, rather, keep your eyes open for opportunities.

Take a long lunch together or go into the office late one day. Lock your office door at lunchtime or other downtimes during the day. Get creative. Think outside of the box and the bedroom.

It could even become a game. Kids are gone—go! Be creative, do something crazy.

If possible, plan a weekend away where you can focus on spending time as a couple, not as co-workers. If money is an issue, especially in the early stages of your business (which it most likely will be), hide out in your house and tell people beforehand you'll be out of town. Have naked movie night, turn off the cell phones, get a copy of the Kama Sutra and let your imaginations go wild!

Other people often see a romantic aura around the idea of running a business with your spouse. At a lunch meeting one day, I mentioned to a colleague that I believe my husband is the best at what he does.

"It is nice to see a wife who is so in love with her husband. It must be romantic to work together," she said.

Ha! How many of you who currently work together just laughed or made some kind of snorting noise when you read her comment? Many of you, I'm sure. But you know it is true: other people see the romance in a couple running a business together. It is heartwarming, charming and inspiring to them. We must be so in love in order to own and operate a business together, they think. Even my own employee says he doesn't know anyone who gets along as well as my husband and I do.

Most people would not want to hang around their spouses for as many hours each day as it takes to run a business together. Think about this before you start your business. Or, if the two of you are already up and running but not quite operating at full steam, keep reading.

Here's another tip: The next time you're too tired to look at your spouse for another minute or if you just want to kill each other, try to imagine the romantic element—the aura of romance—that surrounds your relationship. Try to picture what other people see when they imagine how fascinating it is. Remind yourself how lucky you are to see each other every day, even if you are mad at the moment. Many spouses don't get to spend much time together because they're gone all day working for someone else. The two of you have made a different choice.

Sleep Is Everything It's Cracked Up to Be

Exhaustion is one of the many complaints I heard, and I know this to be true from my own experience as well. Running a business is hard work. In the beginning and even well into the business's middle years, most entrepreneurs spend many waking hours making their business successful. It's worse if you are the main breadwinner for the household. Long hours lead to loss of sleep and lack of energy to do just about anything, let alone sex. It further complicates matters when you toss kids into the mix, especially small children.

My husband and I have two young girls who demand their share of our time. I'm known for passing out on the couch by

10:00 p.m. and being very cranky or even angry if awakened unexpectedly. While I'm more of a morning person, my husband is a night owl. We're not the only ones with this problem; in fact, opposite sleep schedules is a common complaint among many couples, not just those who run a business together.

So, what do you do? Obviously, both of you will have to bend a little on this issue. If you're the night owl, go to bed early once in a while, at the same time as the other person. Set your alarm so you can occasionally be an early bird with your spouse, who is typically up at the crack of dawn. The point is to make an effort. You make giant efforts for your business, so make them for your spouse as well. When all else fails and sex isn't happening as often as you'd like it to, try the "nooner," when both of you are awake!

Managing Both Hats

The second most-common complaint couples mentioned was being mad at a spouse and having a difficult time turning it off when the workday was over. One poor woman even commented she found it hard to flip the switch to the wife role when her spouse yelled at her all day, like a parent might yell at a child.

Wow. That's a challenge. Be careful how you interact. If one person is bossy and assumes a parental role, it will affect your sex life. It's hard to do a 180-degree turn in your head toward mature, loving sex if you feel your partner is treating you like a child.

If it helps, take time to relax after your workday. Talk about family-oriented things, since it is personal time now, even if you don't have kids. Focus on other, home-related subjects you don't typically discuss during the workday.

Above all, remember there are twenty-four hours in a day. Who says you have to have sex at a certain time? Think outside of the box and be playful.

Someone needs to be the initiator. During my interviews, this was typically the male. But whoever it is, be perceptive and be persistent. Don't give up! Chances are, "no" doesn't mean no, it means "not now."

Persevere and keep that spark alive!

Schedule Date Nights on Your Calendar

Every couple should have a regular date night, but I believe this is imperative for couples who work together. Date nights are not only a necessity, they are the lifeblood of any marriage. Relationship experts preach the same thing. For couples who work together, however, date nights can also be rewards for getting through an especially difficult time at work.

Plan them. Date night doesn't have to follow a specific schedule, of course, but you should definitely create some sort of routine. Many couples commented that it does not need to be a grand, spectacular event. Date night simply means time spent together, doing whatever. Go on a walk, get an ice cream cone, see a movie or relax on your deck with a glass of wine. The options are limitless. The point of date night is to have time to reconnect as husband and wife. If you feel comfortable talking about business, go ahead, but keep in mind this is actually time for you to spend on your relationship.

Don't underestimate the power of smaller efforts. If this is not an opportune time for a date night, find other ways to show you're thinking of each other.

My husband does a wonderful job of this. He used to be in a networking group with a local florist. Part of that company's brand or "signature" was to attach a tiny bird to every arrangement that went out the door. Each time my husband sent flowers to me, I kept the little bird. It was charming, and I liked it.

One day he had the bright idea to buy a handful of the birds from the florist, who was touched and impressed with the idea. Then, my husband hid the birds in very clever, sometimes hard-to-find places and waited for me to find them. I eventually found one in my coat pocket, my wallet, on my computer, in my car, inside my jewelry box and even inside the toilet paper roll! He also involved our children in one of the hiding sprees, which served as an excellent example to them.

To this day, discovering a little bird stashed somewhere unexpected is still one of my favorite things my husband can do for me. ... Just the sight of a little bird makes me happy. And even though it barely cost a thing, it shows he is thinking of me.

It's these small efforts that make all the difference. What can your small effort be?

Mine is to leave him notes and send silly text messages. I used to get him a giant, smiley-face cookie for no reason, just out of the blue.

What are some things that make your spouse smile? What small effort can you do? Even if it's an email he or she isn't expecting, a little thought goes a long way. Clearly, money is tight during your business's start-up phase, so become inventive. Make dinner, light a candle, dance in your living room. Buy a song on iTunes and sneak it onto your spouse's iPod. Rent the first movie you ever saw together, pop popcorn and enjoy each other's company. Sit on a swing, hold hands and watch the clouds roll by.

Set little rules if you think it will help. I interviewed a couple who had a bedtime rule. In this case, the wife was the night owl and would work well into the night. Consequently, they did not often go to bed at the same time. Choosing to head off potential problems, they agreed that when the husband went to bed, the wife had an hour at the most to finish what she was doing before joining him. That way, they were still going to bed together at almost the same time each night. Another couple with the same problem always goes to bed together at the same time on date night—even if their plans include nothing else but going to sleep.

As a couple, implement little rules so you can give more attention to your relationship in a variety of meaningful ways. What does it for you? Here are some suggestions.

5 Great Ideas to Enhance the Mood:

1. **Flowers at unexpected times**

2. **Date night**

3. **Weekend getaway, even if it is not out of town**

4. **Naked movie night—when kids are asleep or gone, of course!**

5. **Your own, private wine-tasting event**

What will work for you? Remember to be imaginative and have fun!

Meet Horvath and Gan—Home Improvement and Landscape Experts

Lee Horvath and Christy Gan own a home improvement and landscaping company, now celebrating its tenth year. They met when she started working for a company he managed, which supplied—not surprisingly—materials to homeowners and contractors for home improvement and landscaping. Four years later, Lee, who was definitely gifted in those two areas, went into business for himself. Christy continued to work at another job but was also very involved in running Lee's business.

Needless to say, maintaining a balance between two jobs and a home life was stressful. Sex and intimacy were not high on the list of priorities. Their personal lives grew stressful and the marriage suffered.

"Life just got too overwhelming," Christy said. "I was too exhausted, and I simply didn't have enough time for the kids or for Lee."

Finally, they looked at the problem and decided Christy should leave her other job so she could devote all her time to their company. Suddenly, they had their home life back, their family time more intact and their sex life soared!

With both of them focused on the same company, they worked in tandem. They also shifted the division of labor at home by hiring a cleaning lady, which meant Christy got more sleep and Lee was more involved with the fun projects around the house he had never had a chance to do. The business's income grew, too, because they were both able to better focus on their company when the home front—and the bedroom—were taken care of.

Lee and Christy recommend trying to keep the frequency of your intimate relations the same *after* you start your business as it was *before*. If you don't, the relationship will suffer. Make sure sex is a priority, the couple emphasized, and do as many of the same types of intimate activities you enjoyed together before you started the business.

They even go so far as to recommend a couple explore and enjoy the sexual aspect of their relationship in the morning. "That way, you won't have a chance to avoid it in the evening, just in case you're mad at each other by the end of the day!" they laughed. Lee and Christy also advise making love regardless of either person's mood, saying it's a great stress reliever and helps make the tense times less so.

Good advice, guys. After all, it is hard to be stressed and mad when you're naked!

Soul-Searching Questions

How do you move into spouse mode so you can reconnect with each other at the end of the day? What activities do you and your spouse enjoy that are not business-related?

_____

_____

_____

_____

_____

_____

_____

_____

_____

_____

_____

_____

Let's talk about priorities. On a scale of 1 to 10, with 10 being the highest, where do you rate sex? When was the last time you were the one to initiate romance?

_____

_____

_____

_____

_____

_____

_____

_____

_____

_____

_____

_____

_____

If you're already running a business together, how has your sex life changed since you opened your business? Are you both happy with those changes?

_____

_____

_____

_____

_____

_____

_____

_____

_____

_____

_____

_____

What are some ways you can unwind after a bad day? What types of activities put you in a good mood? Can you do any of these activities together? If not, do you each appreciate the other's need to do an unwinding activity alone?

_____

_____

_____

_____

_____

_____

_____

_____

_____

_____

_____

When was the last time you went on a date together? What are smaller efforts that cost little or no money that you can do for your spouse? What types of things make your spouse smile? (Think of my little birds.)

_____

_____

_____

_____

_____

_____

_____

_____

_____

_____

_____

_____

Is your spouse nearby? Is anyone else around? What are you going to do in the next ten minutes? I suggest you set this book down, find your spouse and pounce!

Chapter
Five

I knew it was time
to send my daughter to preschool
when I turned around to find
she had escaped my office
to go outside and play on the beach!

Apryl Saricioglu, manager of C Properties

Who Is Picking Up the Kids?

The Balancing Act

When people work as employees for someone else, all too often their day consists of briefly seeing their kids in the morning and then for a few short hours at night. When you and your spouse run your own business, on the other hand, you both have a wonderful opportunity to escape that rat-race life and to bring balance to your work and personal lives.

However, no one said this would be easy. With your freedom comes the responsibility of managing the schedules of your entire family and juggling things so that you can actually spend time together, instead of falling into the trap of narrowly focusing on your business all the time.

Fortunately, with both you and your spouse working in tandem on the business, you already have a leg up on making this juggling act work well.

Learn to Juggle

My oldest daughter taught my husband, Marcel, and me that working together was absolutely imperative if we both wanted to keep our sanity. Once she arrived in our lives, we suddenly had three people's needs and schedules to take into account, and everything became more complicated. The better we could work together to help each other plan our days, the smoother things went. The similarities between raising children and running a business with your spouse are amazing. And when you actually do both, the two are often so intertwined that there isn't much of a distinction between them.

In our situation, it quickly became clear that not only were we going to need to work harder at our business, but also at our time management skills. In addition to ourselves, we now had to keep track of a little one.

From our own experience, plus that of the couples I interviewed, I have several ideas to help you manage your business and family time more effectively.

Use your company meetings—even if these meetings consist of only the two of you—to determine who is in charge of delivering the kids to their activities and whose turn it is to play chauffeur or keep a watchful eye on the child.

Remember when I said that raising children and running a business are amazingly similar? Here's your opportunity to make efficient use of everyone's time by doing both!

My husband and I make it a standard part of our company meetings to discuss the family calendar. Who is picking up the kids, who is dropping them off, which extra-curricular activities they need to get to—this should all be discussed and divided as equally as possible between the two of you. Make it a part of your normal schedule to be involved with your kids, in spite of your work schedules. They will appreciate you for it, and you will be glad you made time.

One common method of maintaining order on your family's calendar is to use different colors for different types of events. For example, I use the color purple for my business appointments (my company logo is purple!), the color blue for things I need to do for household needs and the color pink for events for my girls. Marcel, on the other hand, only uses two colors to distinguish between business and personal activities. Figure out a method that works best for you, but keep in mind that the simple use of colors can really help keep things straight at a quick glance.

You can also find large calendars that incorporate stickers and other ways to decorate the calendar to differentiate events of the household. For example, some stickers represent holidays and others school events. Writing in business meetings on this calendar helps all family members know when mom and dad need to work and should therefore be disturbed as little as possible—they can't be available for extra carpool duty, or a trip to the store for supplies needed to finish that social studies report due in the morning. Kids love colorful decorations and stickers, so they feel they are being included in the business and are more likely to cooperate.

On the other hand, no matter how carefully you plan, life happens. Boy, does it ever! I will cover this topic more extensively in chapter six, but it is worth mentioning now since kids often propel us into that "life happens" mode. Their needs, their health, their activities, their schoolwork, their teenage hormones—all conspire against your carefully balanced schedule, or so it can seem.

At the same time that these unexpected and often unwelcome demands rush at you, you are also ultimately responsible for handling the day-to-day operations and any crises that may arise at work. Let's face it, you don't really have a choice: you and your spouse must remain flexible and available for last-minute changes to your plans, no matter which direction they come from.

The key to surviving these "life happens" situations is to stay in frequent communication with each other. Use technology to your benefit by moving beyond traditional phone calls, for example, and send text messages when you know your spouse is tied up and can't talk on the phone. Or temporarily move your company meetings (those for the two of you) during an especially busy week to after business hours—early in the morning or late at night, if you must. The secret is to stay flexible and to communicate.

Support, Support, Support!

Obviously, there will be times when you need a little help. It is absolutely imperative to have a reliable support system in place. Just like you count on your banker, accountant and attorney to be there for your business, another integral part of your team is someone who can take care of your children. You need to know that you can rely on someone to watch them while the two of you are handling business matters.

Certainly, if you live near your family, get them on board with your plans. Recruit them to help with childcare, but explain that you will likely need help at odd times too and sometimes on short notice. Not everyone, however, is lucky enough to have family around. Many couples I interviewed did not have family in the area, so they had to get creative in finding childcare.

A great idea was to approach students at local universities. Placing an ad for nursing, physical therapy, or education majors was the number one pick among the couples I spoke with. These students often need part-time or summer jobs, and they typically love being around kids. They are high-energy, creative and usually trustworthy and responsible individuals.

My church membership has also yielded several awesome babysitters, which works great, since I am a big fan of knowing the babysitters' parents. I guess getting ratted on to your parents if you do a bad job is very motivating to these young people! Aside from that, I'll typically see the babysitter at church every week, so I'll know in advance what kind of person he or she is. This method of finding quality childcare has worked fabulously for me every time.

Deciding to trust someone to watch your kids is definitely something you and your spouse should do together. Sit down and write a job description, highlighting what type of person each of you wants for this job. Besides the attributes you want your childcare provider to role model for your kids, you should also think about what kind of personal attributes you would want in an employee at your business. After all, this childcare provider is an employee of sorts. You'd likely want someone who acts maturely and is reliable, for example, so be sure to think in terms of "employee."

When you find a prospective caregiver, interview this person just as you would an employee. Help him or her understand that this job is, in actuality, to serve as an employee of your business, even though he or she won't be on the business's payroll. Without that individual, however, you and your spouse cannot work and make money, so the provider is integral to your business. Both you and your spouse must explain how your business works and how the need for a reliable person to help with the kids is important; this isn't just some standard babysitting gig. You two are not just going to dinner—you are running a business.

On the flip side, make sure you treat your childcare provider with all the respect you'd give an employee.

If both of you discuss this with the childcare provider, your joint presence will emphasize the importance of his or her role. You're also more likely to cover everything. Plus, the employee will feel more comfortable asking either of you questions later, if needed.

Should the Kids Get the Corner Office?

Bringing children to the office is something many of us entrepreneurs have needed to do at one point or another. Some couples even do this every day, which can make it challenging to keep young ones occupied.

Giving them their own space at the office is something every set of parent entrepreneurs should consider. I have seen self-employed moms with everything you can possibly imagine in their office, from a crib to the child's own desk and computer. If you have an office outside of the home, what creative ways can you incorporate a space just for your kids?

Our kids were just beyond the toddler stage by the time we had an office outside of our home. We made sure they had a desk with cubbies to store toys, coloring books and anything else we thought would hold their interest. The Slaughters, whom we interviewed in chapter one, sometimes use their office's physical therapy equipment to occupy their kids and grandkids! Other couples have had a small office serve as a mini-playroom or entertainment center with a television and video games. One couple even brought in their kids' sleeping bags and popcorn for movie nights if they needed to work late. Having these things in place is imperative for couples who work together. There will be times when babysitters aren't available but work still needs to get done, so be prepared.

The point is to give them their own space, even if it is just a corner of your own office. That way, they feel more included in the business. If you meet with resistance, you can always say, "Let's go to our office to play." That statement always made my girls feel more important. They knew that when I picked them up from school, we would go to our office, have a snack, and then they would play with toys or the computer until it was time to come home. Having them there was often the only choice I had if my support system was not available.

This scenario is especially true of really young ones. They need to see you more often, so creating a fun and whimsical environment to comfortably hang around in is important.

Ideas to Keep Toddlers Quietly Occupied:

- **Coloring books, crayons, markers**

- **Blocks**

- **Puzzles**

Ideas to Keep Elementary Ages Quietly Occupied:

- **Board games, card games**

- **Books**

- **Legos**

Ideas To Keep Middle-School Ages Quietly Occupied:

- **Laptop/iPad/iPod Touch**

- **Scrapbooking, or other art-related activity**

- **Comic books or other books, or homework**

The number one thing I recommend for all ages is the iPod Touch. You can get free or nearly free apps that satisfy any age for hours. If you insist that this or any other fascinating children's activity remain at your workplace, even your most reluctant child will be eager to go to mom and dad's workplace.

Your list will change as your child grows and discovers new interests. The important thing is to find out what your child currently loves and provide a space for it in your workplace.

You Always Wanted an Assistant

Marcel made the official jump to a full-time entrepreneur when our first daughter was six months old. You can imagine my horror when I realized we were no longer going to have a steady paycheck, yet we had a brand-new baby in the house. I have to admit, however, his timing was impeccable. He knew he wanted a flexible schedule so he could be around his little girl and experience all those things that only happen when children are very young. We worked hard to schedule client appointments around the availability of daycare and each other's schedules. Our daughter was also an extremely good baby, so we could—and did—take her everywhere. Marcel even brought her to a few client appointments, which actually won him brownie points with the clients!

When done properly, this could work in your favor. In our case, our clients loved interacting with our kids and watching them grow up. But this won't work for everyone, so proceed with caution. Some clients or prospects will turn up their noses at your apparent lack of professionalism. No matter how quiet and well-behaved your children may be, other business professionals simply don't want them around. Period. So, learn to read your clients and do what is best for everyone.

It is also a good idea to include your kids in the errands you need to run for your business. It not only allows both of you to spend more time with them, but also helps them feel like they are part of the business. For example, we took our girls with us to networking events, ribbon-cutting ceremonies and numerous other events, so our children could see what other business owners do. Consequently, our girls love attending these functions and have gotten to know a lot of other business owners in the community.

Some couples will take their kids on shopping trips for the business. Others have taken their children to trade expos. At first, you might think your kids would find these trips boring, but you will likely be surprised at how much your kids are interested in how your business operates. Some couples use their kids as greeters in their stores, even going so far as to instruct them to occupy customers' children so the adults can concentrate on shopping and, thus, spend more money!

Whether you do it on a regular basis or hardly ever, at some point, you will be forced to take your kids with you to a business meeting or other professional event. After all, you have to keep the business moving ahead, and work needs to get done, despite those "life happens" days. If you do it correctly, by properly planning and preparing, you can turn it into an outing for the family and a great experience for everyone. So, work together and hopefully you can make it fun too!

Their Little Piece of the Pie

I think most parents dream of passing the results of their hard work on to their children. Some business owners choose to bring their children to the office for that reason alone. Many couples I interviewed commented on not only how much they enjoyed having their children in their workplace, but also how much the kids learned from those experiences.

Children of entrepreneurs grow up knowing that their parents have had to work hard for what they have. Every generation agrees that it is important for younger people to fully grasp the meaning of the old saying, "money does not grow on trees."

In our case, our kids have never known us to have another job. They believed for years that everyone owns their own business. At the dinner table several years ago, my oldest talked about running her own restaurant someday, as if it was a natural and common thing to do, a foregone conclusion.

I asked, "You've decided to run your own business?"

"Of course," she replied. "You and daddy do it, so I can too."

Wow. I sat a little straighter after she said that, proud of what Marcel and I had accomplished and instilled in our children.

There is a special bond created when you include your children in what you are doing. Many of my couples commented that even if their kids did not eventually follow in their footsteps, their children always had an appreciation for what mom and dad were doing. The longer the kids were around the business, the more they wanted to be a part of it and watch it grow. Consequently, the parents often included the kids in business decisions and even brainstorming sessions for the business's future growth as the children got older.

Let your children be a part of what you have created, if they're interested. They will appreciate what you've accomplished and the incumbent benefits so much more if they have been included in the process.

Make Time for Family

It's easy to lose focus on your family when you start a business, but running that business with your spouse can make it easier to keep your life balanced. Even with your spouse's help and commitment to that balance, however, you will still have to work at it. Unfortunately, the flip side of the coin is also true: with both of you involved in the business, you might both lose that precious balance, to the detriment of your kids. So make family time a priority.

It can be as simple as looking up from your computer to give someone a smile or a hug, or taking a break for an hour to color with your kids. In the long term, you need to believe family time is just as important as work time. If you glance at your color-coded calendar and the whole thing is purple, that is your clue to add some pink. Schedule a family outing to the zoo, for example, or take your kids to a movie. Or simply stay at home: your kids will appreciate you hanging out with them.

That is the beauty of being your own boss. Schedule your time whenever possible so you work during their naps, their playdates, while they're in school or pursuing other activities.

**5 Things You Can Do with Your Kids
to Get Them Involved:**

1. Introduce them to your clients/customers when appropriate. Your children need to learn that these are the people who spend money with you (the same money you use to buy crayons and movie tickets, for example), and, consequently, these people need to feel welcome and appreciated.

2. Have them help you check in inventory because learning organizational skills is important.

3. Have the older kids proofread your blog. It will teach them more about what you do and help their grammar skills at the same time.

4. Brainstorm new ideas for the business with your kids. Your kids are more helpful and insightful than you think, and they can bring a fresh perspective.

5. Have them shadow good employees periodically, which helps your children see what goes on when you are not around. It can also be a form of positive recognition for your employees.

Meet the Karagiannis—Restaurant Owners

Dino and Jules Karagiannis have been married for twenty-three years. Ten years into their marriage, Jules came on board with Dino and his family to run the family restaurant. Dino had grown up in the family-restaurant environment, so he was comfortable with his role. Jules, however, was new to running a business. One of the first challenges she encountered was how to handle both the kids and the business.

Dino thought having their daughters at the restaurant with them made perfect sense. Jules felt differently, however, especially when their girls were very young. Instead, she called on her support system: Dino's parents and sisters and her own sisters, who absolutely adored the Karagiannis' children. Jules was lucky to have a great support system in place, with family living close by. Most of the time, either an aunt or the grandparents were available to keep the girls occupied while Jules and Dino dealt with the restaurant's day-to-day operations.

Today, however, Jules warns parents to not take too much advantage of a great support system. "In the beginning, it was great. My kids were the first grandkids on both sides of the family, so everyone was overjoyed to spend time with them. After a while, though, I learned the aunts were growing a little resentful of having to watch my kids so often, and that the aunts' childcare commitments cut into their own lives and activities. Consequently, I made other arrangements from time to time so I wouldn't take advantage of their generosity. Still, we are Greek, so family taking care of family is very important to all of us."

As the girls grew older, Dino put them to work in the kitchen, coatroom, storage room—wherever they were big enough to handle the job. "Kids' hands are the perfect size for making a salad!" he laughed.

The couple's children went from playing in the playpen in the back office to bussing tables and eventually hosting and bartending. As it turned out, the children have been included in most aspects of the business since they were infants.

"It really was just a way of life for us," said Jules. "The girls went with their grandfather or their dad to the meat market or fish market or whatever errand had to be done that day. When they were young, they played in the back office, got themselves a snack in the kitchen, and even lay down for a nap in one of the back booths. You do what you have to do to survive in the early years. I feel like the kids have been wearing aprons forever!"

Jules and Dino both expressed how helpful it has been to have their children at the restaurant. Although they are not sure if the girls will take over the business someday, the couple is positive that their daughters care about it. The girls want to help improve the business, Jules explained, and they feel like they really do have a vested interest in it.

"I am so proud when they make suggestions and try to help us resolve problems or issues we are having," she beamed. "For instance, when they see a problem with our computer system, they often have it solved before they even let me know about it. It shows me that they are really paying attention to what is going on around them, and that they have the confidence to speak up, take action and make a difference in the business."

She added, "The only thing we ever had to watch out for was taking them to other restaurants. They thought it was normal practice to wander into kitchens and help themselves to things in the fridge!"

More proof that you still have to watch the little stinkers.

Soul-Searching Questions

Is it possible for you to take your child to work with you sometimes? Would it upset your clients if your child came with you to appointments? What creative ways can you think of to work around this?

_____

_____

_____

_____

_____

_____

_____

_____

_____

_____

_____

Are you able to change your schedule to accommodate your children's activities? Do you have an arrangement with your spouse to get them where they need to be, but that also allows each of you to finish your work commitments?

_____

_____

_____

_____

_____

_____

_____

_____

_____

_____

_____

Do you have family nearby who can be part of your childcare support system? If not, what questions do you have in place to hire someone you can trust to watch your children? Write a description of the perfect person for the job. List ten questions that are important to you and your spouse and that you will ask everyone you interview.

_____

_____

_____

_____

_____

_____

_____

_____

_____

_____

If you have an office outside of the home, is there a space you can allocate and equip just for the kids? What items do you need to obtain to set up such a space? Is it still feasible for you to work if they get noisy?

_____

_____

_____

_____

_____

_____

_____

_____

_____

_____

_____

What variety of ways can you make your kids part of your company? Can they go on errands with you? Can you assign them their own set of responsibilities when they are in the office? Do they understand what kind of business you do and how they can help?

_____

_____

_____

_____

_____

_____

_____

_____

_____

_____

_____

_____

Chapter
Six

One of the perks is not having to fake an interest in what my husband does for a living!

Christy Gan, owner of Lee's Services, Inc.

Fringe Benefits

Time for the Perks

We have been discussing what needs to happen to make your business successful, how to overcome stumbling blocks that edge from your business and into your marriage, and other family-related topics that spill over into the business. By now, I wouldn't blame you if you were thinking, "Why am I doing this again?" I know I've asked myself that question many times!

Yet every job comes with some fringe benefits. It would not be a fun job if it didn't, right? So what are those fringe benefits of working with your spouse? What makes all of this apparent chaos worthwhile?

This was one of my favorite questions when I interviewed my couples. They had so many wonderful, heartwarming things to share—and they always smiled when they talked about these benefits. Things like the ability to brainstorm together, schedule family time without having to check with a "boss," adapt to life's curveballs and, most of all, this awesome bond they'd formed by building something so incredible together.

In fact, in every instance, in every interview, the smiles on their faces when I asked about this topic told me they felt everything was worthwhile. Personally, I think the list of fringe benefits far outweighs anything good spouses could get by working separately or for someone else.

Two Minds Are Better Than One

Brainstorming together was one of the top items on the list. The ability to do this with a spouse was exciting to them, and it is to me too, I must say. Actually, both my husband and I get positively giddy when we work together to come up with ideas and solutions for our business. We think big, we get enthusiastic about the future—and we always want to start on our ideas right away. Sometimes, we'll move into brainstorming mode when we are just plain stuck on a problem. We are each other's "go-to guy" for any problem.

Brainstorming is more fun with two brains involved. I have used brainstorming since my corporate days, but I find it much more enjoyable when I can do it with my spouse. We sit down, tackle an obstacle and work on it until we're bouncing ideas around like mad. Some of them, I will admit, are just downright crazy.

Naming this book was a huge brainstorming session that lasted a long time. We started out by sharing ideas via our cell phones and text messaging. Finally, we parked ourselves on the couch and came up with fabulous ideas in person. It was a blast!

We have done this with many aspects of our business. Naming the business, designing newsletters, coming up with creative ways to attract more clients, figuring out how to deal with ornery clients—you name it. Brainstorming is a typical task for all business owners, but it's much more fulfilling when your spouse is not only involved but also has the same vested interest in the business that you do.

Maybe part of the excitement is that I don't have to go home and explain to my husband this awesome, creative idea I just had and then make him see how exceptionally smart I am to have come up with it. He already knows!

However, and I think most of my couples agree, the power of simply accomplishing something with your spouse during a brainstorming session is incredibly satisfying. Think about it.

You have just solved your world's problem, and you got to do it with your spouse. It's empowering, and you feel like you can take on the world.

"Vacation, all I ever wanted ..."

It should go without saying that when you are your own boss and you work primarily with your spouse, taking time off together gets easier. I didn't say it was completely easy; leaving your business is always difficult. But when you work with your spouse, you really only have to be concerned about one family's schedule instead of throwing your hat in the ring with other co-workers and their busy schedules as well.

I used to work for a government office and I was the low man on the totem pole. Vacation time for me was slim pickings. I got what I got and that was the way it was. I always had to wait for someone else to be in the office before I could go anywhere—we had to have coverage at all times.

Working with your spouse can make things so much easier. If you want to leave together, you make it so. It may take a lot of maneuvering, but you can do it when you really want to.

When you just need a moment to yourself, away from work, you can ask your spouse to cover for you, and vice versa. No more checking with other people or following unwieldy protocols. That alone is a huge perk.

Unfortunately, time off is not always for a great reason. Life happens. But, there again, working with your spouse is a fantastic perk in these situations. He or she completely understands why this is a "life happens" moment.

When you can call your husband because of a family situation, he'll cover for you. If someone is sick, you go. Someone needs your help for whatever reason, so you go. My mother, for example, is disabled and on any given Tuesday, I may need to make a quick dash to all sorts of medical facilities on her behalf, or even with her in tow. Having this kind of perk allows for that.

As we've discussed, life happens. You cannot control it. Isn't it nice that when you work with your spouse, you can tag team your efforts?

We have often changed our schedules on the fly, to deal not only with family members, but with employees' schedules, too. It happens all the time.

I agree that sometimes scheduling can become tricky, but aren't you glad you and your spouse are the ones who call the shots? If one of you needs to go, the other will always have your back. This is the perk of working together I think I would miss the most. I love being in charge of my schedule and my life and knowing I have the ability to change it when I need to. Not only for me, but for my family.

What Binds You Together

Describing how couples form a strong bond is something that I find hard to put into words. As I said in an earlier chapter, running a business with your spouse is like raising a child together. You care for it, nurture it and it would be nothing without you. For those of you with children, think about what you went through, or are going through, to bring them up in the world. Now think about how much you are going through, or would go through, if you started your own business. Just like a baby, it needs constant attention, nurturing, love and support.

I often wonder how can people start businesses without the help and involvement of their spouse. It happens all the time, yet I feel that running a business is, well, intimate. It takes all your heart, soul, determination, perseverance and love. How can you possibly take on an undertaking such as this without the involvement of your spouse? You married this person, so why would you not want him or her to also be involved in some way in your own little place in the world? In fact, all of the couples I interviewed mentioned this special bond, which actually makes their marriages stronger.

Running your business really is like having that extra child in the room—the child that needs your constant attention. You created it and you get to work it together. How awesome is that? You've probably also noticed that with this bond comes the admiration and respect for the strengths you may never have known the other person had. You are put into situations you would never be in if you weren't running a business together. Thus, you're both learning what you didn't know the other had in them, which reinforces the relationship bond.

My advice is to feed off each other's energy and skill, as well as from the business. Just like I discovered unknown strengths in my husband when our first child came along, I also discovered more as our business grew. This especially happens when you are creating ideas from scratch together. Your ideas and the bond I am talking about are just like a child: made from scratch, together. Your bond is undeniable, and it is a part of both of you.

Life Happens

Let's look more closely at what exactly goes down when "life happens."

In reality, most of us have absolutely no clue what kind of curveball life is going to throw us on any given day. We have no idea what is coming or when.

Strong people that we are, we could likely deal with it on our own if we had to, but when we work with our spouse, those curveballs are so much easier to see, to react to and triumph over. This ability to roll with life is my most-cherished perk of working with my spouse, and I believe many people feel the same. It's worth another look.

Having a partner at home and at work who can help keep you on track is invaluable. Your special someone is watching out for you, helping you remember details when you are stressed, and who remains focused on keeping the money coming in if you are not able to do so, thanks to whichever unpleasant thing just landed in your lap. And we all know these obstacles derailing you from your daily (or weekly ... or longer) To Do list arise in both our personal and business lives from time to time. Most likely, you've bailed out your spouse when he or she had to dodge a bullet and unexpectedly shift attention to a demanding situation, so you know it works both ways.

Like most couples, we've been through our tough times. One bittersweet Thursday, the day our second baby was born, we learned my father-in-law had finally given up his fight with cancer.

At the time, and so soon after giving birth, it just about destroyed me. How could we be so happy and so sad at the same time?

How could we even contemplate running a business and caring about other people?

Yet how could we not?

We were self-employed, with a new baby and a funeral to plan, all at the same time. I cannot describe to you the grief and joy we felt on that day—in between answering clients' phone calls and doing what we had to do to run the business.

My husband was a rock and stood strong for both of us—how, to this day, I am not sure. But, life happens. We roll with it. Even though I was recovering from having a baby, I still made sure I was there for him in his grief, and to appreciate the challenging reality he had as he dealt with clients and our first-born.

These days, one of my favorite sayings is that "you never can tell what will happen on any given Thursday," but I am so glad that my husband will be with me to handle what happens on my crisis Thursdays.

5 Curveballs Life Can Throw at You

1. **Family health issues—your own, your spouse's, your children's**

2. **Aging, needy parents, or a death in the family**

3. **Economic downturns or loss of savings**

4. Home remodeling challenges, or unexpected repairs to your home or vehicle

5. An exciting but unplanned opportunity for you or your family, e.g., travel, a pet, continuing education

Do any of these sound familiar? Are you and your spouse prepared—as well as anyone can be—to deal with these situations?

Obviously, there will be more challenges that are unique to your situation and family. Running a business typically means you never stop thinking about it, but if you need to, at least there are two of you to tackle the unexpected situations.

You can't stop life, but you have some control over how you handle it when you work with your spouse.

And sometimes, you actually have a crack at those curveballs.

Meet the Lohmanns—Water Specialists

Talk about curveballs! Dan and Julie Lohmann did not plan to have their own business. They each had other jobs when they were first married.

Unfortunately, Julie was diagnosed with breast cancer. Taking it in stride, they dealt with it the best they could until Julie had to quit her job. Dan, in the process of taking care of her, lost his job as well. (I am happy to report that now, nine years later, Julie is cancer free.)

During that time of hardship, grief, and fear, however, they stumbled upon a unique business opportunity: running a water purification business. Today, the Lohmanns install water softeners and reverse osmosis systems to people who are drinking poor water, something near and dear to Julie and Dan's heart. After what the two of them went through to keep Julie alive, they want everyone to be as healthy as possible.

But how did they get from being jobless to running a successful business together?

In their earlier days, Julie had always wanted to go to nursing school and Dan was intent on finding another job. But life happens.

When I interviewed this couple, I was struck by how empowered they felt, no matter what type of situation they were in. They did not simply lie down and take the crappy deal that cancer was offering. Instead, they became their own boss, so they could call the shots and determine when it was a good time to work and when they had to take a break for Julie.

"In the beginning, I will admit, it was hard to get into the mindset of the entrepreneur," Julie said. "It was feast or famine all the time until we learned how the money would roll in and we could then plan our lives a little better. But it was really hard to swallow in the beginning. We had to quickly draw on each other's strengths to get good at bringing in more business so we could plan our finances better."

But now, she would not have it any other way. "I feel so blessed that I can be with my kids when they are sick, deal with my own health issues and actually plan a vacation without having to answer to someone else."

Dan agrees. His number one priority is his family. Who better than himself or Julie to determine when someone needs help or time off to deal with the family?

Julie also mentioned the importance of respecting each other's strengths—of being aware they exist and appreciating how useful they can be. Julie, for example, is known for her philanthropy and Dan is known for his "MacGyver" tendencies to fix everything with a paperclip and duct tape. They each have the unique ability to connect well and easily with others. They would not have fully realized this about each other or benefitted from it if life had not put them in the situation they were in and they had dealt with it by becoming entrepreneurs.

Dan and Julie know that life can turn on a dime, and when you are in control of your work life, especially with your spouse, you can deal with those curveballs—and maybe even some fastballs.

Soul-Searching Questions

Name the extra benefits that you enjoy most about being self-employed with your spouse, or would likely enjoy if you were self-employed.

_____

_____

_____

_____

_____

_____

_____

_____

_____

_____

_____

How often do you brainstorm with your spouse? What kinds of things do you brainstorm about? What other topics can you add to this list?

_____

_____

_____

_____

_____

_____

_____

_____

_____

_____

_____

_____

Who plans the vacations in your family? Is taking a vacation easier to do when you control when you and your spouse can leave?

_____

_____

_____

_____

_____

_____

_____

_____

_____

_____

_____

_____

List your top five vacation destinations. What things do you want to do on those vacations?

_____

_____

_____

_____

_____

_____

_____

_____

_____

_____

_____

_____

_____

If your family was to suffer a tragedy or loss, or had to deal with an important life event, who is in charge of changing the schedule to accommodate this? Is that an easy or hard task?

_____

_____

_____

_____

_____

_____

_____

_____

_____

_____

_____

_____

What are you happy you no longer have to think about or do because you now work with your spouse? What are some obstacles you still need to overcome?

_____

_____

_____

_____

_____

_____

_____

_____

_____

_____

_____

_____

_____

_____

Being realistic, if both of you were unable to work, do you have someone in mind and prepared who can run the business while you are away? Do you have a formal agreement with this person to protect your business?

_____

_____

_____

_____

_____

_____

_____

_____

_____

_____

Chapter
Seven

The mistakes are yours and the glories are yours.

Alice Welch, former owner of E.J. Welch

Happily Ever After

Pearls of Wisdom

So far, we have revealed that we need to be in it to win it, how to divide our wonderful talents so roles are clear, the importance of avoiding the snowball of crabbiness, how to shift from the boardroom to the bedroom, ideas on dealing with the kiddos, and reiterating why we run a business with our spouse in the first place.

Believe it or not, this simply sets the foundation for a successful business. You and your spouse are now properly positioned to discover the vast world of entrepreneurial knowledge that awaits you, including the many things they don't teach you in school that can really help your business stay afloat and other things the two of you will learn on the fly.

Life happens. You have to learn how to deal with it the best you can and, in business, profit from it. So, drawing from my experience with my husband, as well as what I learned from the couples I interviewed, here are some of my final thoughts and idea nuggets.

Have a Mentor

The reason I wrote this book in the first place was to share with other couples just starting out what my husband and I have learned and how we learned it. We want to share this knowledge so other couples will not need to live through the same mistakes we made.

With that said, the most important lesson is to seek and learn from mentors. We cannot stress enough how crucial mentors are, both before you start a business together and while you are running it. If you haven't found a good mentor or two yet, I urge you to do so immediately.

Reaching out to someone else—and admitting you need help—is not easy. Do it anyway. Don't delay.

When we first started our business, I was afraid to approach other business owners about how they handled certain situations.

I assumed what was going on in their businesses was definitely none of my business, and I imagined they'd be shocked if I got up the courage to ask questions.

Marcel, on the other hand, was not shy about it. He has a very calming way of approaching people and thus found out a lot of information. Thank God he did! We made it easier on ourselves by joining our local chamber of commerce early on. There we met other business owners and not only gained clients, but friends too. With these friendships came the courage to ask and that is when we discovered ... other entrepreneurs love to help!

We quickly figured out when to ask, what to ask and whom to ask—especially after my husband and I disagreed on the types of things I mentioned in earlier chapters.

When you work together, it is easy to assume one or both of you will figure out any given problem. But sometimes, you just can't. At those times, asking for help comes in very handy.

After several years had passed, I was able to return the favor to new entrepreneurs I met while I was networking. My husband has done the same. It is one of the core teachings in my coaching business. Share your network, your knowledge and your compassion, and you will make a difference.

Winners Aren't Born; They're Coached

Networking events not only facilitate meeting people, they are also educational. It was there that I first learned about business coaches. I was instantly in awe of such a prospect. Wow—there are people who help business owners for a living? How incredible is that? I could finally turn to someone—without worrying if I was a bother or too inquisitive—when my husband and I could not figure something out or simply didn't know what we should do. Obstacles we'd faced with getting more clients, managing cash flow issues, and dealing with clients who did not pay on time—these immediately sprang to mind. These concerns were important, too, because they greatly affected not only our company, but our home life, too, since most of our income at that time was tied to the business.

Business coaches, I learned, have many different styles and programs. Some coaches are famous and are practically household names. Others aren't. How do you choose which coach and program is right for you?

The answer is that it depends on your current situation. Think about where you are with your business's development. Where do you see yourself going? Where do you feel stuck?

Getting more clients was our challenge in the beginning. There is an old saying: "when the pupil is ready, the master will appear."

And, just like that, we met a coach who guided us through what we needed for our business in a way that we both understood, have since applied to other businesses and still use today.

Sadly, I see couples hesitate to hire someone to help them through rough patches in their business. Their fear of spending money stops them from overcoming the barriers to becoming truly successful. One or both of them is getting caught up in how the bills will be paid. Sometimes even the fear of success stops them from actually going out and getting the job done. I have heard countless times, "my spouse is afraid to spend money and grow too fast." When I hear either of these comments, I encourage people to set their pride aside and ask for help. I encourage them to stop that way of thinking. Just like marriages can sometimes need a marriage counselor, businesses need a coach.

Don't think you know everything there is to know. I guarantee you don't. If you are at all like Marcel and I were when we first started out, you don't even know what you don't know! So surround yourself with people who can teach you what you need to learn, whether that means hiring a business coach or simply talking with the right people at networking events.

Surround yourself with people you want to emulate—successful people. Find other couples who run businesses together and ask them if you can interview them. Learn what they've learned.

Implement what they've done successfully and makes sense for your business.

Be supportive if your spouse is the one who wants to seek help. Remember, an unbiased point of view is incredibly helpful when the two of you are stuck on a problem or cannot agree on how to solve an issue. Use these unbiased people as mentors and coaches to help you.

5 Ways to Find a Mentor

1. **Ask local chamber of commerce members; they're often willing to help others.**

2. **Join online groups—LinkedIn is a good place to start.**

3. **Participate in networking groups, such as Business Network International (BNI).**

4. **Attend business seminars, where you'll often find like-minded people.**

5. **Ask friends and family to introduce you to people they know.**

Your Very Own Board of Directors

Another suggestion is to form your own board of directors. My husband and I decided only three years ago to have our own board of directors for our business. I wish we had done it sooner. We picked smart, successful people with a variety of expertise, and we selected them from people we had done business with or because of their track record with mutual clients. We not only assembled financial planners, accountants and bankers, of course, but also people who, quite simply, knew what they were doing. If they ran a successful business and had a strong background, we wanted to feed off that knowledge. And we knew they were willing—even eager—to share.

When we invited them to be on our board, they all expressed honor and a desire to help whenever they could. We chose not to have everyone attend actual, face-to-face board meetings, but left it be more informal instead. We send monthly progress updates via email, call them with one-on-one questions if it pertains to their field of expertise, and even keep in contact when nothing much is going on.

The other members know each other, and don't necessarily communicate with each other about us, but often leave things open for discussion in emails so we can all learn and contribute.

Our way of thanking them for their time and expertise is referring business to them. All of this works very well, and we feel good knowing there are people in our corner who look out for us if we need help or have questions on how to move forward with something.

I encourage you to do the same for your business. Assemble a board of people you can trust to have your back in the business world.

Interview as Many People as Possible

One thing I wish I had done is more research about owning a business in the first place—what is it really like, for instance.

Think about how long you take to make a decision on buying a house, or the research you do before buying a car or some other major purchase. This is no different. You would not take a job offer from someone without investigating the salary, benefits or hours, would you? Why not apply the same principles to opening your own business? Do market research ahead of time. Ask questions. You don't know what you don't know, so keep asking questions. They will lead to more questions and more opportunities for people to give you advice.

Specifically, I wish I had sought other entrepreneurs and asked such questions as these:

> Why do you get up to do this every day?
>
> Why did you choose this profession?
>
> What is the one thing you wish you could do over again?

Little did I realize back then how easy this task actually is. Most people love to talk about themselves, right? Use that to your benefit.

Interview other business owners you already know about how they got where they are. Dive into your chosen industry and make friends before you even start your business. If you can afford it, apprentice somewhere so you can truly learn what it is like, before you commit yourself, your spouse and your family to this new venture.

5 Questions to Ask Other (Non-competing) Entrepreneurs

1. **What are your experiences with other service professionals, (e.g., accountants, lawyers, technology consultants, bankers), and who do you recommend and why?**

2. **Have you run into any problems, such as sign ordinances, when dealing with local government entities?**

3. **Who are the top three to five people I should meet right away, and can you help facilitate those meetings?**

4. **With the two of you working together, how do you juggle family and home life? How is it different from not working together?**

5. What was your experience with start-up capital, and what are your thoughts on it? What is a comfortable amount to finance?

Money, Money, Money, Money

A common concern I heard from nearly everyone I interviewed, including my husband, was how to successfully manage money. Most people also said that money was the thing they most often fought about, and, in comparison, other problems seemed minor.

Nearly all of my couples confessed that, while they had properly assigned only one person to be in charge of the finances, the other person would often have no clue as to the state of those finances. Everyone agreed this had led to problems.

What advice did they offer?

- **Communicate with each other often on the state of the finances.**

- **If neither of you is good with money and projecting income and expenses—*go find someone who is!***

- **Make sure you have the same financial goals and are equally willing to take risks.**

- **Be honest with yourself and each other. Don't go along with whatever your spouse wants, just to make**

him or her happy. That type of behavior only leads to frustration, worry and stress, which neither of you need.

I was guilty of this last habit for a long time. Starting a business was my husband's dream, and I wanted to be supportive in every way. I saw the writing on the wall, however, when we were headed toward financial hardship. I mentioned my concerns to him, and he usually replied, "Everything will be all right." But it wasn't. And I could have stopped it if I hadn't been so determined to make my husband happy.

In hindsight, he would have been happier if I had done something to stop the money problems when I could have. We have had to learn the hard way that the "love factor" in a spousal-run business will not let us ignore or minimize such tough topics as money.

The number one thing that will test your passion—for your business or marriage—is your money running out. Make sure you communicate if there is a problem or a surplus, so you can deal with each situation appropriately, and together. Don't allow a financial issue to sneak up on you or your spouse. Do not run your business through rose-colored glasses. Create a plan ahead of time and talk about it regularly.

Meet the Browns—Technology Experts

Marcel and yours truly are the Brown family, and I remember
like it was yesterday when he first talked seriously about starting
a business. He had been thinking about it, apparently, for several
years before that, which was when he started helping people after-
hours with their computer issues. I was always very supportive
of his dream, even though I had no idea how it was going to
change our lives.

He had always been great with computers and, during his
childhood, he quickly emerged as a prodigy. Later, he studied
computers in college. Marcel even built one of the first Internet
service providers (ISPs) for the area we lived in—with no
training. He just figured it out on his own. I have to admit, in the
beginning, when he was helping people on the side, it was nice
to have some extra cash around the house.

It quickly became a full-blown enterprise, however. Marcel's
clients passed his name around to their clients and friends, and
we soon faced the decision about doing this full-time. Could we
actually create a company, based on his skills?

We did what no one should ever do: We jumped. We saved only
three months' salary and said to ourselves, "If all else fails,
Marcel will go back to work for someone else in a tech job
somewhere." In those days, that would have been very easy to

do, because there were plenty of jobs for someone like him with an enormous amount of skill. This is not the case today, and we don't recommend anyone adopting this attitude.

We learned the hard way about how a business works: marketing, advertising, networking, day-to-day operations, accounts receivable, how to manage finances, legal issues, accounting issues—you name it.

We came from the fields of technology and interior design. Unfortunately, we only had a basic knowledge of business, and, as we soon found out, not nearly enough knowledge between the two of us to understand what was about to happen. We were only relying on our strengths and not paying attention to our weaknesses.

I quickly discovered that marketing was absolutely critical. Marketing our business became my job and it had to happen on a daily basis, which was hard to do because I still had a full-time job and a newborn in the house. We put a lot of effort into marketing because we knew its importance but also because of a very simple reason—we wanted to eat. I dove into the field of marketing every chance I got. I bought every book you can imagine, read every blog, and started taking part in marketing events. Luckily for me, I like to talk, so networking and meeting people came naturally. It quickly became evident that I was the best one to do the talking. My husband was a very heads-down, get-the-job-done, make-the-client-happy type of guy. I was, of course, left to deal with the business that happens on a daily basis: inventory management, keeping the finances under control, making sure all the bills were paid—a not-so-easy task.

I managed to keep my full-time job until my company ran into hard economic times. I survived two downsizings but not the third. I lost my job the day after I learned our second child was coming. It was scary, but, at the same time, it was the push we needed to really tackle this thing we had created head on. I had no choice but to dive in and give it everything I had, because we had to keep paying the bills, as does everyone.

With the entire household suddenly relying on our company's income, we added a lot of pressure to our lives, but we somehow made it through. We made mistakes, of course, but we learned from them. One mistake I particularly remember is our decision to let my husband be in charge of advertising. He was so excited about the business that he advertised in every avenue he could think of! Holy cow, did that cost us dearly! After that, he was fired from making any and all marketing decisions.

It's not just our mistakes that we learned from; accomplishing great things was instructional, memorable and motivating. For example, as the business grew, I discovered I excelled at networking, marketing and coaching, and I enjoyed it, too. I became known as "the person who knew everyone," because I relentlessly attended networking events and grew to truly love that aspect of running a business. If I had never become an entrepreneur, I would never have embraced my gifts and used them to make a living. And you wouldn't have this book!

Soul-Searching Questions

Why do you get up to do this every day? Why did you choose
this profession? What is the one thing you wish you could do
over again?

_____

_____

_____

_____

_____

_____

_____

_____

_____

_____

_____

_____

Are there other business owners in the community that you both look up to? Who are they? Are they people you can call and ask for advice? If not, what would it take to start a relationship with them?

_____

_____

_____

_____

_____

_____

_____

_____

_____

_____

_____

Have you considered hiring a business coach? Are you both willing to participate in coaching sessions and listen to advice from someone outside of your company? Do you have a hand-picked board of directors to keep your best interest at heart?

_____

_____

_____

_____

_____

_____

_____

_____

_____

_____

_____

Do you and your spouse have the same outlook on money? Are you risk-takers or conservative or somewhere in between? Are you both willing to spend money on your business, even at the expense of giving up something for your family?

_____

_____

_____

_____

_____

_____

_____

_____

_____

_____

_____

Are you willing to be honest with each other if the dream is not going well from a financial standpoint? If you should fall on hard times, how far are you willing to take your family's sacrifices in order to keep the business running?

_____

_____

_____

_____

_____

_____

_____

_____

_____

_____

_____

_____

Conclusion

And So It Begins, or Continues, with You ...

This book is my gift to you. Running a business is hard, being married is hard at times and combining the two can seem like a crazy thing to do. But, as you have seen from the couples I featured in this book and from my own experience, not only is it possible to run a business with your spouse and stay happily married, it can also be extremely rewarding. There is no one else in the world with whom I would choose to run a business.

Most people decide to become entrepreneurs because they love what they do and want to have more fun doing it. So why not choose to do this with the person you have the most fun with? Why not pick the person whom you know is always there to help, no matter what?

Grab your dream, grab your family and take them along for the ride, but, above all, have fun with it—together.

About the Author

Danelle Brown is the founder and president of Queen Bee Consulting and a certified Book Yourself Solid business coach. She specializes in showing owners of family- and couple-owned businesses how to get more clients than they can handle. Danelle is known for turning ordinary businesses into extraordinary ones.

Along with her husband, Marcel, she is also the owner and marketing director for MB Tech, Inc., in Glen Carbon, Illinois, which provides technology consulting to small businesses and individuals. Using her husband's gift for technology and her innate creativity to reach her various audiences through non-traditional means, Danelle runs several websites and blogs devoted to business topics. She has also earned the nicknames "master networker" and "Queen Bee of Connections" in her geographic and online communities.

After receiving her degree in interior design in 1997, Danelle went on to work with several prestigious, family-owned design firms in St. Louis, Missouri. At about the same time, she and Marcel started a home-based business. Because of her extensive marketing and promotional efforts and the time she's spent "learning how the world works," as she describes it, they continue to grow their company, not only through smart marketing efforts, but also through client retention and word of mouth.

Danelle's specialties include social media, business coaching, marketing, and accountability programs. She instructs and assists business owners with implementing their social media strategies and marketing plans. She's also an expert at connecting people and demonstrating the art of networking. In her blog and on her Facebook page, she often writes about the networking experiences and things she's learned from talking with other business owners. Not surprisingly, she adds new followers every day. Danelle has also coordinated production of MB Tech's newsletter, Technology Bytes, for more than three years and continues to grow it through word of mouth. Additionally, Danelle counsels and guides small business owners who meet each month in Mastermind groups she hosts.

Danelle and Marcel have two young girls, Isabella and Elena. The Browns are extremely active in their children's private school, Lahr-Well Academy. When she is not working or being a mom, Danelle enjoys cooking, wine tasting and traveling.

For more information or to contact Danelle, visit her websites at www.queenbeeconsulting.com or www.soulmateproprietors.com.

16.95   12/8/16.

LONGWOOD PUBLIC LIBRARY
800 Middle Country Road
Middle Island, NY 11953
(631) 924-6400
longwoodlibrary.org

LIBRARY HOURS

Monday-Friday	9:30 a.m. - 9:00 p.m.
Saturday	9:30 a.m. - 5:00 p.m.
Sunday (Sept-June)	1:00 p.m. - 5:00 p.m.

CPSIA information can be obtained
at www.ICGtesting.com
Printed in the USA
BVOW04s2149011216
469554BV00015B/68/P

9 780982 925706